Elegant Choices, Healing Choices

Marsha Sinetar

Elegant Choices, Healing Choices

PAULIST PRESS
New York / Mahwah, N.J.

Cover Photograph: Katherine P. Comstock

Library of Congress Cataloging-in-Publication Data

Sinetar, Marsha.
    Elegant choices, healing choices/Marsha Sinetar.
       p. cm.
    Bibliography: p.
    ISBN 0-8091-3010-6 (pbk.):$7.95 (est.)
    1. Self-actualization (Psychology) 2. Choice (Psychology)
I. Title.
BF637.S4S56 1988
158'.1—dc19

                            88-21785
                               CIP

Published by Paulist Press
997 Macarthur Boulevard
Mahwah, New Jersey 07430

Printed and bound in the
United States of America

Contents

THIS BOOK IS DEDICATED TO RAYMOND J. SINETAR:
MY DEAR FRIEND, AFTER ALL THESE YEARS

What we commonly call man—the eating, drinking, planting, counting man, does not—as we know him—represent himself, but misrepresents himself. Him we do not respect. But the soul, whose organ he is, would he let it appear through his action, would make our knees bend. When it breathes through his intellect it is genius. When it breathes through his will it is virtue. When it flows through his affection it is love.

Ralph Waldo Emerson

Preface

I am unusually fortunate to have such consistent, professional and competent colleagues. Pam Bacci did all the word-processing for the manuscript of this book. She has an eagle-eye for detail, works speedily, works nights and weekends in order to finish chapters quickly. She seems to sense my eagerness for an almost immediate turn-around. I cannot thank Pam enough. My editor, Dianne Molvig, is tough: she is completely fearless when it comes to cutting, red-penciling and reorganizing my chapter drafts. As a result she is a great help, and always improves upon what I write. Both she and Georgia Mandakas, my editor at Paulist Press, are kind and willing enough to tell me when I'm vague or have missed the mark.

Our team, not I alone, puts a book together. I thank all three friends for working around my travel schedule, for keeping my whereabouts in mind as they work so that chapters can be sent to me wherever I am. Each of us lives in different states, so I probably am indebted to the express mail service too.

A word of thanks is due Paulist Press: Father Lynch, Don Brophy, Bob Byrns and Hugh Lally in particular, are people with whom I communicate regularly. They like what I write and have from the beginning. Paulist Press was my first publisher and has held my hand through the publication of three books. A starting writer couldn't find more supportive, reliable and honorable people to work with and I am grateful.

Introduction

Ever the optimist, I believe each of us can grow whole as persons. More optimistic still, I believe each of us can use our daily choices, even the most insignificant ones, to help us along this path. That is the theme of this book. Yet, I have decidedly not written a book about *what* to do. Rather I yielded to my intense interest in the psychology of human health so as to present some thoughts about how our choices help us *be*, and become optimally healthy. Since choice, per se, reflects who and what we are, as individuals, I wanted to investigate the way in which our choices can refine us and develop us into actualized, fruitful, enduring persons.

Each choice says something about us, says something to us, imprints a message in and on us. These messages further our good or defeat it. Each and every thing you and I do has the power to knit us up on the inside where we are split, separated, fragmented. This, in essence, is what I mean when I write that choices can *heal*.

Then there is another thing: my use of the word *elegant*. I chose that word because it precisely describes that inner refinement, that personal grace, that effortlessness, that lovely naturalness commonly embodied by supremely well-developed persons. This, in essence, is what I mean when I write that choice can be *elegant*. The elegant choice enables us to become increasingly individuated: more of what we know ourselves to be, on the inside, at the core of our most noble self,

1

about whom Walt Whitman wrote, "the soul . . . would [we] let it appear through our actions, would make our knees bend." I have not used the word elegant to connote such things as "good taste," or any other socio-economically determined indicator of status, style or conduct.

But I would be untruthful if I said that an appreciation of aesthetics did not play a part in my choice of words or content. I have always been personally moved by beauty in all its forms. I experience beauty as healing. So I wrote this book as a way to think about how we ourselves can be made more beautiful inwardly, as persons, through our everyday choices. A short personal anecdote may pinpoint the way I have experimented with my interest in this entire topic:

In the earliest days of my professional life, when I was a brand new primary teacher working with first grade, inner city, ghetto children, I saw that beauty—in any form—affected the children in a positive, wholesome way. I spent what then seemed like vast sums on flowers: long-stemmed roses, and violet-blue irises, when I could find them, just to watch the children's reaction to these lovely gifts of nature. Fresh flowers like these, which many of the students had never seen in such abundance, made my class behave better. Their transformation was amazing. At first, because it is my own nature to love such things, I thought I was imagining. I spoke to my fellow-teachers about my observations and they assured me I was dreaming.

Yet something deeper was at play. The addition of fresh flowers to the classroom, good music, beautiful art work and photography, a well-turned phrase in speech or writing, guest speakers who demonstrated a regal bearing or a noble train of thought always impressed the students. They would come up after school, or during recess, to touch an item on display, to speak shyly to a guest, or to say, the way only a child can, "Thank you. I like this." They blossomed. And so did I.

In due course, their conduct improved along subtle lines. They paid greater attention to the *way* they did things. They were careful with their papers. They wanted to keep their desks, their pencils, their composition and art work clean and pretty. While their spontaneity and enthusiasm remained fresh and lively, they grew sensitive to a high personal standard, as if trying to approximate the natural standards of beauty so often brought to the classroom. They were proud of their work. More important, they were proud of themselves. They taught me a great deal about how any and all touches of beauty benefit people both physically and emotionally.

My more recent research into the values and life-choices of actualizing adults, and my work with corporate clients (among the best educated, brightest and most creative people in the country, certainly in the top three percent of these categories) has reinforced my belief that beauty heals. The children I first worked with were six and seven years old. The adults I now work with are between thirty and seventy years old. Not one person, not a single one, has ever failed to improve when he or she improved the way daily choices were made.

I now know there is something in our nature, as a species, which responds in like fashion to beauty, to truth—another aspect of what I and others call "the good"—to all those values, universally held sacred by mankind: honor, courage, love, nobility or intent and the like. These values help us, grow us into better persons, speak to us of God. Yet, while these values have little to do with material affluence, my sense is they do have much to do with an *affluent spirit*. This spirit, in turn, is really what wholeness is all about.

As we elevate and educate ourselves to the deeper qualities, the values, the aesthetics of choice, we can improve ourselves substantively. We can learn, for example, to make the best possible choices, even when there are very poor alternatives open to us. As we sensitize ourselves to our own underlying motives, habit patterns and to why and how we choose, then we can teach ourselves to make productive choices *as a way of life*. Perhaps the Zen Buddhists, masters in this art, have been saying this all along—for centuries. Most of us are slow learners in such things.

The thing to remember, again and again, is that we always observe ourselves, even if we do so unconsciously. We always, each and every time, notice when we choose wisely. We also notice, each and every time, when our choices go against our interior grain. The truly significant factor, underlying this most personal observation, is that we also reward and punish ourselves, each and every time, for our choices.

Each time we choose in an elevated way, so that we and our highest interior virtues are supported by the choice, we "register" this, as the psychoanalyst Karen Horney taught, and we give ourselves credit. When we choose poorly, we register this too and we punish ourselves. This notion of "registration" has become a hallmark of my methodology. The concept also undergirds much of the way in which I present the material in this book, although I do not discuss this directly. Related materials, my professional and university-based lectures, explain my methods more fully, and I am currently preparing training materials for qualified professionals who are interested in working along these lines.

Chapter One defines the phrase "elegant choice," and explains what I mean by healing choices. I have stressed the psychological components of healing, since that is my area of expertise. However, in the last chapter I also attempt to examine how daily choice, specifically those choices which build our sense of self-control and give us more control over our life, can actually promote *physical healing*. Always and increasingly I find myself encouraging people to develop in themselves what psychiatrist Robert Lindner called "positive rebellion."

Always and increasingly I urge people to work slowly, conservatively and with a gentle hand. We human beings can take any method and shoot ourselves in the foot with it and I, for one, do not want to contribute to the bloodshed. My own toes have a few, thankfully not too many, scrapes on them.

Chapters Two and Three describe a growth factor I call "self-definition." I'm not certain if the phrase is original, probably not, but I've not heard it before. I've used both real-life and literary characters to demonstrate the way in which self-definitional ability heals us. By living well-defined lives, by creating the context of our life, by asserting ourselves at the exact point of our idiosyncrasies and life-purposes, we become more alive. Bland adjustment is the kiss of death to life. Theologians might call this bland adjustment "accidie." The word means the sin of failing to do with our life what we know intuitively we can do. I say that choices which build a bulwark against "accidie," choices which let us live as we know intuitively we must, heal us; these give us more life.

In these early chapters I also suggest that by choosing to involve ourselves with superordinate goals (values and activities beyond ourselves) we grow more vital. In the mid-section of the book I examine how choices can help us accept our fear, overcome it. An extension of this idea is outlined in the chapter called "A Fighting Spirit Till the End," where I try to show that by choosing to fight, when it is necessary, for our best selves, for our privacy, for our well-being and self-respect, we can build physical strength and endurance even in aging.

I trust the last chapter properly underscores my bias that, ultimately, love is our only answer. We must love ourselves, and forgive others—thus loving them, in the final analysis—even when we see ourselves choosing as vulnerable, flawed beings. If we can simply accept ourselves when we know we have chosen unwisely, we can grow into fully human beings.

I have not developed the bridge between choice and aesthetics, and am hoping that some fine-art instructor some-where will explore this link; I'm sure there are parallels between fine art and fine choice, but this book didn't seem the place, nor do I have the background, to pursue the idea.

A related, more urgent side-issue is the one of children, improved learning and beauty which I mentioned too briefly in this introduction. There are important educational ramifi-cations to the whole realm of choice-making, personal devel-opment and the enhancement of self-esteem. Perhaps there are current important research studies underway to examine how art, music, poetry or dance impact learning. Having been in private practice for almost eight years now and thus out of the mainstream of public instruction, I am unaware of these. If, as I suggest, our simplest choices can help us develop as whole persons, are we doing enough, on a national basis, to teach very young children about the subtle dimensions of their own daily choices? Are we, for instance, teaching primary students that their choices have the power to help them feel good about themselves? Can we improve early childhood education to make children more conscious about themselves as choicemak-ers? Should we devote more funds to beautifying inner city schools, simultaneously teaching children about the value of beauty to their minds and souls? And should we provide sim-ilar instruction to parents and teachers so they can be better role models in this area? I believe so, but leave such matters to teachers and other community professionals in the hopes they will be interested.

I invite readers to write to me, as I have invited their re-sponse in the past. The letters I receive are of great interest to me. Whenever possible I attempt to write back, although sometimes now this is hard to do. I find the personal corre-spondence valuable to my work and to my life since letters, with good ideas, enthusiasm, and practical, common sense, now come from all over the world. I find this amazing and wonderful and thank anyone in advance for taking the time to send a word of encouragement to me.

Finally, I want to add that as I wrote this book I discovered many lessons I need to learn. I practice daily.

Elegant Choices

> People have (with the help of conventions) oriented all their
> solutions toward the easy and toward the easiest side of the
> easy; but it is clear that we must hold to what is difficult.
>
> Rainer Maria Rilke,
> *Letters to a Young Poet*

We humans so easily resist our own good. From within ourselves, from our most basic drives and urges, come strong forces
that take us in perversely inelegant directions. Repeatedly we
sabotage our long-term good, acting as if we were adversaries to
the very life, joy and vitality we desperately crave. We become
addicted to the wrong foods, or we use chemical substances for
energy or to blanket our awareness of the things in our life that
don't work. We avoid those persons who might be helpful to us,
and we move closer to those toxic to our long-term good. Deeper
still, in unconscious regions of our souls, we fear our own
strength and talent and goodness, which, when developed fully,
make us visible, distinctive, powerful and fully responsible to
take on more of the things we now avoid.

Yet, certain people do move forward. They inspire, lead
and help us by their courage and honesty, and by the way they
direct their energies and commitments. For the most part these
persons are actualizing—growing toward their best selves—
and they teach us how to grow, as well. They demonstrate,
through their lives and actions, what is healthiest, most attrac-

tive and meaningful. By their way of being, their values and their choices—and this is what this book is about—they point the way to complete personhood.

This is how I see it: people who know how to choose in refined, graceful or pleasingly superior ways are people who grow inwardly into healthier, wholesome beings. If we study the elements of their choosing—the qualities of their choices, their motivations, the traits that such choices bring about and cultivate—we can equip ourselves with new strengths, ideas and actions for our own choices. Perhaps right choosing comes first, like a grace, from an inward place of readiness within ourselves. Maybe the outer choice is symbolic of an interior healing that allows the positive movement of choice to take place. One thing for sure, *by paying attention* to our choices—and to the stuckness we feel if we can't yet make a move in the direction we want, or to the liberation we're feeling when we know we're choosing rightly—we not only learn about ourselves, but plant the seeds for further development. The more healthful our choices—and I'm going to call these *elegant choices*—the greater healing we receive in all ranges of life.

While it truly is my intent to be very practical in this whole discussion, I should say that in general each human choice has both *motive* and *quality* to it. That is, we usually have reasons for the things we do, even though we may not consciously know what these are. And our decisions and actions have within them inherent qualities which—at least in the perceptions and interpretations of the chooser—can be known, even demonstrated outwardly, in the choice itself.

WHAT IS MEANT BY ELEGANT CHOICES

By elegant choices, I mean those options that are, by and large, tending toward truth, beauty, honor, courage—in other words, choices that are life-supporting both in motive and in quality. By the same token, our avoidance of elegant choices will be life-defeating or self-defeating, as the opening paragraphs suggest. When we back away from the truth, when we go toward what is to us, morally low instead of elevated, when we choose from motives of self-loathing, our sense of self-respect is harmed and diminished. At some level, however subterranean it might be, we are always watching ourselves, always monitoring our thoughts, words and our deeds.

When choosing between telling the truth and fabricating something, avoiding truth will seem inelegant to us. In a choice between two activities—one done in a slothful way, the other done in a more disciplined, orderly fashion—the slothfully done task will seem inelegant to us. In choosing between a fear-driven choice and one which is motivated by faith—in ourselves, in the other, in God, or in a higher order of things—the fearful choice is the one that will undo us *in our own eyes*. At some level of consciousness we will say to ourselves, "I've behaved badly. I've chosen like a coward. I *am* a coward." What I will discuss in this book, illustrate in different ways, is how we might correct such contaminated, unproductive self-evaluations.

At the same time we must move cautiously and with the utmost *nonjudgment*, as it relates both to ourselves and to others. In some cases, what looks like sloth may not be. Going slow, laying low, taking it easy may simply mean we're resting, or that we're building up energy reserves for another activity. This is certainly true for a weary traveler, which I so often have been, tired after a long, hectic trip, napping for a few days, or just puttering around the house, leaving work or a messy, mail-covered desk for another, more energized day. Artists report that after a burst of creative, intense output, they go into a kind of physical torpor while creating anew on unconscious levels. What looks like a lie may actually be our intended kindness, as when we're asked for our opinion about someone's appearance, and—trying to spare that person's feelings—duck the truth. Honesty would say, "You look terrible." Kindness softens the blow, skirts the facts—yes, even lies.

Thus, one of my ground rules in this discussion is to hold firm to the idea that only the individual concerned can really know whether his or her choice is elegant. Only that individual can know about the fear or faith levels of motivation; only the chooser knows whether what looks, on the surface, to be a fearful step or an unattractive one is courageous, decent or beautiful. Readiness also matters: the child who backs away from a confrontation will not think as poorly of himself as the adult who sees herself in a pattern of avoidance. In the final analysis, the relativity of each choice (its context, the person involved, the specific issues) underlies our self-evaluation. Having said all that, we are ever alert to ourselves in these matters, ever watching, ever awake. We register our choices, for good or bad, and measure ourselves by what we notice ourselves doing.

When my editor first read the title of this book, she cautioned me to be certain to say that the elegant choice was not the fussy or superficially materialistic choice. Most of us tend, I suppose, to think of elegance as something reserved for society matrons, fashion experts and upper socio-economic consumer groups. However, to me, *elegant* means refinement, grace, distinction, polish, finish. There is nothing at all in the word that connotes social class, yet each person—whatever his or her life circumstances—can grow in refinement. This is after all no more than a purification of what we are at our best. In my eyes, even an old building—say an ancient church, or deteriorating barn—has an elegance to it.

This development process, it occurs to me, is also what we do when we develop into full persons—we refine ourselves, gain greater understanding of what we are, attempt to use our best judgment and discernment for our choices and in our life.

As we shall see in later chapters, as the phrase "elegant choice" relates to the aging process, and to the type of choice that enables us to live vitally, what we notice is that the elegant choice is often the *harder choice.*

Yet while the elegant choice is not the perfectionistic choice nor necessarily the stylish or trendy one, there may be an aesthetic standard to it. Elegant choice-making has little to do with form or appearance, but—full of paradox and contradiction—such choices often have some measure of propriety and outward aesthetics, however for reasons of *substance*, not form.

The person who retains her grace under pressure, the one who is polite despite being tempted by another's rudeness to sink to rudeness in return, the one who is kind to us even when we are mean, can each be said to have elegance even though their way of dress or manner of speech might be coarse. Once when I fell ill while at a large metropolitan airport, a cleaning woman helped me into the women's lounge so that I might sit down. Her hands were rough upon my arm, she had a toothless smile and her well-worn uniform was wrinkled and slightly soiled. But she was so helpful and comforting I shall always remember her as having enormous "class." In my eyes, she had an elegance, a humanitarian dignity, that the others around me lacked.

A CASE EXAMPLE

A client of mine was depressed and wounded after being fired. The company he worked for, a major airline, had been aggressively acquired by another and he was one of the middle-management victims of this difficult takeover. When I saw him shortly after he'd received the bad news, he looked pale and preoccupied. He said he could hardly get out of bed in the morning.

Despite his usual self-disciplined, productive nature, my client, hurt and suffering, was spiraling downward by making a host of inelegant choices. He looked seedy and disheveled. Perhaps this was his bid to gain sympathy. More likely, he was simply depressed. His appearance was one of the first things to go. I took the liberty of suggesting that he see a clinical therapist, and he revealed that he'd already made the call. But, he added, even the littlest chores at home were hard to cope with, and—having the opening I needed—I began to tell him about my own experiments in healing psychological wounds.

For ten years or so, I'd been developing some techniques to improve self-esteem, and I described the methodology I was using with others. I suggested he try some of these techniques on himself in order to repair himself emotionally. Whereas I thought he'd be cynical, I noticed he actually cheered up as I talked. My client said that my suggestions made sense to him. With that, we jointly planned some steps for him to take that very afternoon and the next morning. Here's what was planned:

Since for the past week he'd been unable to make the bed, and he admitted the sink was brimming with dirty dishes, those were the areas selected. As soon as he returned home that afternoon, he was to change the linens on his bed, launder them immediately, *and* make the bed as perfectly as he could. Groaning, he said he'd do it. More instructions: he was to clean up the kitchen spotlessly, to the best of his ability, as if the King and Queen of England were coming to dinner. Every knife, fork and spoon had to be buffed dry to a lustrous finish, then put away neatly. I told him to stay up later than usual at night if necessary to do the things listed, focusing all his attention on every part of each task and chore.

Before dressing the next day, he was to shave and shower

impeccably and give careful attention to every seemingly un-important detail of his grooming routine. He was to select his favorite outfit to wear to work, even something he'd been sav-ing for a special occasion. This was a special occasion. He was taking himself to work! He was to follow, even embellish, this routine for one week and after that we would meet again and evaluate the results.

When I met with him again the next week, I was startled to see how much better he looked. Color and life had returned to his face. His energy was up. He admitted feeling better and happier, "more like myself," and his new therapist was amazed at how quickly he was responding to treatment. With that bit of positive feedback, we continued mapping out other action-steps he could take on his own behalf. Within three weeks, he was working on his own choice-making plans; within a few more weeks he was out of his other therapy program as well.

Of course, there are persons who do not get better quickly. For every story like this one, there are hundreds of others, conforming pretty much to the details of this plot, wherein people do not feel better. They don't have the energy or the desire to take the more helpful route no matter how hard they try. Perhaps they don't possess the clarity or the stability of mind—given the weight of their burden or the depth of their sadness—to even think about doing such trivial tasks. But, I hasten to add, this man did have the wherewithal to get on with his life. And so do many other people.

I'm stubborn. I know this works when one applies oneself intentionally or has the self-respect to get help (as my client did) while sorting things out. I am not, of course, suggesting that by merely making elegant choices people magically lift out of clinical, psycho-physical depressions, schizophrenias or other severe mental illnesses. Clearly for these cases, psychi-atric and medical intervention is necessary. But I am saying that for most of us—who are not psychiatrically sick, but who nevertheless yearn for a respite from some hurt, who long for a fuller life, who feel ourselves to be growing too slowly in long-sought-after directions of wholeness and selfhood—such actions are uplifting and growth-promoting. Elegant choices produce real and rather rapid development.

I should add quickly that these ideas are not unique, not my private invention, even though the applications may be quaintly my own.

Ancient scriptures teach us that the way to overcome evil is with right action, right thinking, love-in-action. All these are ways of saying the same thing. In the book *The Dhammapada*, the sayings of the Buddha (563–483 B.C.) reveal that he advocated mindfulness, discipline, truth, righteousness. Again and again he taught that freedom, liberation, could be gained only with a quieted mind:

> With single-mindedness,
> the master quells his thoughts,
> He ends their wandering.
> Seated in the cave of the heart,
> He finds freedom.
>
> (Byrom, 1976, p. 13)

The Bible advises in the same way, even providing a formula for our thinking, a prescribed mold for our thoughts. If we wish to follow a healthful path, we must discipline our mental processes. We are told to "think on these things: whatsoever things are true, whatsoever things are just, whatsoever things are of good repute . . . "

Additionally, the most rigorous of psychological teachings offer similar counsel for our conduct. For example, the noted American psychiatrist Fritz Kunkel conceived of a way of behaving he called the "We-feeling." This focuses us, as individuals, on cooperation, service and the cultivation of relationship and empathy between self-and-other. It takes us out of our smaller, egocentric, self-involved self into the world where others can be our main focus.

> Find a way to understand better the unhappiness of someone oppressed by racial prejudice or social injustice. Look for the shy person to whom you can be friendly. Give a lift to your tired fellow-worker. Let your imagination lead you into some We-feeling response to those far away. . . . These are but a fraction of the possibilities which may be discovered [if you observe life and others carefully]. (Kunkel, 1940)

These choices—using the We-feeling; keeping our thoughts on positive, beneficial things; acting single-mindedly and with love—restore inner peace and happiness. Let us make no mistake here: we *can* choose what to think, how to feel, what to do. Conscious choice itself is elegant. All of these involve elegant choices: the selection of the good, the helpful, the positive or the loving over their opposites.

There seem to be only a few ways to meet growth, change or life-challenges. Two of them are: to numb ourselves to the entire experience, become unconscious or helplessly depressed (and this is bound to happen sometimes, no matter how we handle ourselves) *or*, as we find ourselves able, meet the challenge head-on. By this I mean we function, as well as we are able, here and now. We move as much as we are able in the direction of health, beauty, orderliness and stewardship—the care of, compassion for or giving to the other. We grow as much as we are able, at this moment now, toward courage, truthfulness and self-respect. At the very least, we support ourselves psychically *wherever* we are.

In other words, the elegant choice consists of our *motivation* to move in a healthful, helpful, life-supporting direction as well

as it consists of our actual choice or *action*. Whether we are ready
to take one step or many matters less than our general direction of
motives and choices. Which way are we headed? Toward health
and wholeness, or toward self-pity, withdrawal, neuroticism
and malfunction? What do we say to ourselves when we see we
are stuck? Do we allow ourselves human emotion and fallibility
or demand robust perfection even during a crisis?

What heals us, what begins our self-renewal—thus, I believe, promoting actualization—can be just some tiny act. We
are simply required to do what we *can* do, here and now, at
this moment in time. Even the right thought can help if we're
too discouraged, too exhausted, to act. The mere flick of an eye
in the elegant direction, coupled with our intent to bring our
more whole self into being, begins our gradual move into more
productive ways of choosing.

If we can but attend to ordinary home or body mainte-
nances when we feel wretched—clean the sink, scrub ourselves
properly when bathing, put away clothes, make a sturdy,
hearty soup—we help our mood. What should you do when
you feel low? What should you do today? Start small, stay conscious, put your best effort, your highest virtue in your elementary choices. This is elegant. This heals.

There is, in us, a *part-that-knows* what we should do. John
Cantwell-Kiley in his book *Self-Rescue* tells us the part-that-
knows is none other than our whole self. This part in us is intact, a king, has power. It reverses our impoverished state—*if*
we simply follow its directives.

Another way of saying the same thing is from the ancient
book of the *Samurai*. The aphorism instructs us on the value of
doing small things well.

> . . . if one is but secure at the foundation, he will not be
> pained by departure from minor details or affairs that are
> contrary to expectation. But in the end, the details of a

matter are important. The right and wrong of one's way of doing things are found in trivial matters. (Tsunetomo, 1979, p. 55)

How we do things counts. Quality of action matters—not just in the world of commerce, where American industry is slowly learning the truth of this—but also as individuals. *How* we do things counts for us. There is a part of us that knows this, has always known it, and this part watches. When our choice has an aesthetic to it—according to a standard of virtue within us—healing starts.

Beauty heals. Truth heals. Coherence and order heal. Courage, valor, honor—all of these qualities heal us. And by "heal" I mean *make whole*, patch up any split in ourselves that still exists. When we are strongly centered and connected to Self, our spontaneous choices are more likely to be true, courageous and attractive. I have written of this at length already (Sinetar, 1985), but some short reinforcement seems appropriate at this point.

This split, or separation from Self, may be what the theologians refer to when they speak of "sin." Some theologians are keen on having us feel that our "sin" is more serious, a horrible stain that no prayer, gnashing of teeth or good works will heal. But surely a part of our transgression—if there is any—may be largely innocent, unconscious, even if manifested through our will.

The separation from self is what causes us to act against our best interests. When disconnected, fear dominates, and self-doubt, self-flagellation and untruthfulness abound. It is then that we betray ourselves, go against the part-that-knows—because we are acting from a point of self-betrayal. While fragmented, our deficits control us. We cannot be counted upon to think or act rightly any more than can an infant always act responsibly.

A case in point: a client of mine is a marvelously efficient executive secretary. She rarely makes errors. She balances all types of activities smoothly. She runs a tight ship. She is functionally excellent. All those are good and "perfect" things. She didn't get where she is—practically administering a multi-national corporate headquarters—by accident. One day, however, while setting up the travel schedule for the company president, she really bumbled. She actually booked him (and he actually *went*) on the company jet to the wrong city for a major presentation. Horrified at what she had done, she spiraled downward in her self-opinion. Finally, after two weeks of self-flagellation she came to talk to me.

By that time, she'd made several other, though lesser, errors. She burst into tears as soon as the door shut, telling me she was suffering from fatigue, burnout, shame. "I'm in the wrong job, and hurting my boss by staying. I'm going to quit," she sobbed. Of course, we discussed her options. But, on a deeper level, I was struck by something else, namely her unwillingness to forgive herself for the original mistake. Her remorse and embarrassment, while understandable, seemed extreme. I asked her if she might just possibly be making new errors, even contemplating resigning, as her way of punishing herself for sending her boss to never-never-land. Immediately she froze, expressionless with recognition of the rightness of that remark.

Instantly she saw how she was punishing herself for being human. With this realization she snapped into a better connection, a healthier relationship with her rational, responsible self. The connection came, in part, because awareness itself has healing properties—both in the emotional realms and, I believe, in the physical as well.

With her initial insights, she knew quitting was not her answer. All she had ever needed to do was forgive herself for her mistake and get on with her work. Her brutally harsh idea that she should never make a mistake, that she should strive to be immune from human imperfection, stemmed from an equally brutal and conditional self-evaluation wherein she could only accept herself when she was "perfect."

There was, of course, serious repair work to be done, most of it revolving around her perfectionism, her impossible-to-reach standards of flawless performance and the low self-esteem that drove her to such striving. Being human, she needed to more graciously accept her foibles. Our conversation was a first step in that direction, while through the more time-consuming work (i.e., her learning to stay centered and self-approving even when she made mistakes) she saw she could manage on her own.

When we are in right relationship with our whole self, our choices spontaneously help us. The elegant choice maintains us in a place of right action. Within ourselves we feel secure. Our best self moves us forward, in an ever-progressive direction of our truest potential; we unfold naturally, and with a sort of silent, effortless grace.

Our own wholeness, integration and actualization knits us back together when we fall away, bonds us with tiny life-sustaining stitches whenever and wherever we are separated. Elegant choice moves us to a timeless, spaceless place inside where we are healed. At that point even our errors, physical ailments and human flaws no longer wedge us open. Progressively, we experience a blissful sort of safety, a subjective indwelling joy, despite the ups and downs of life.

Abraham Maslow put it into crisp and clear terms while describing how the eternal virtues appear alongside the healthiest persons' choice-making:

> Such people, when they feel strong, if really free choice is possible, tend spontaneously to choose the true rather than the false, good rather than evil, beauty rather than ugli-

ness, integration rather than dissociation, joy rather than
sorrow, aliveness rather than deadness, uniqueness rather
than stereotypy, and so on . . . (Maslow, 1962, p. 158)

Maslow, of course, was presenting his thesis: that healthy
people tend to choose what generally is good for them. He
maintained that we could trust healthy, actualizing people to
select things that are to their (and to others') benefit. He said
repeatedly that healthy people are better choosers than unhealthy people.

My thesis is this: *that we grow healthier, stronger, more actualized if, when and to the degree we select things that are in line with
beauty, truth, integration, order, joy, aliveness, life, virtue, love and
so on.* In other words, the elegant choice itself helps us become
whole—we can utilize our choices as yet another self-actualization tool. This observation comes from my own research,
work and writings which, over the years, have been attempts
to study and help develop healthy choosers. From the case his-
tories of creative, productive, actualizing adults, I've seen that
they transform themselves, as well as their circumstances, because of their elegant choices. They become healthier for making the choice; these acts, decisions and values empower them
inwardly while enabling them externally.

I do not suggest this is the easy way. Yet it is simple: an
uncomplicated, principled way of thinking about productive
choice-making, especially as it relates to us when we're fearful,
in toxic relationships, or upsets of all kinds. This way nudges
us to a tougher stance in decision-making. The depressed can
(if they will, and often they truly do need help to will it) make
their beds, bathe or groom themselves properly, or do whatever little thing is in line with their good. The angry can (if
they will, and sometimes they need help to will it) calm themselves and act responsibly. The addicted can (if they will, and
usually they need help in willing it) stop their addictive

choices. This is the troublesome choice, the narrow path less traveled. But it works on our behalf. In fact, when we really stop to think about it, what alternatives do we have?

This more rigorous path is the route to our salvation, although paradoxically it may require the quiet activity of prayer, meditation, life-simplification or solitary discipline. The good news is that it works. The bad news is that choosing elegantly is sometimes almost impossible to do. Either we simply can't get out of bed when we want to—the body-chemistry, our internal motor, is simply "off." Or we just don't have the courage to tell the truth or confront a certain bothersome person. Or we lack the will to discipline ourselves the way we know we should. Or we don't yet possess the love inside to stand up for ourselves or others. This happens. And this too shall pass.

Merely accepting this simple truth about ourselves—that we are stuck—*is* the elegant choice, the best way to get un-stuck. The part-that-knows knows if we need outside help after our initial self-acceptance.

Accepting what we *are* at a given point, rather than backing away, is truthful, gets us closer to reality, is the more wholesome attitude and choice. Usually things get better from that moment on. The fact is that there are different forces at work in all of us. Wasn't it St. Paul who admitted that he couldn't seem to do the thing he would do? If he did things continually that he didn't really want to do, cannot we admit this failing too without inordinate self-blame? Often we cannot because, in fact, we don't want to improve our lot.

Dr. Garth Wood, a contemporary English psychiatrist, has coined the term "Moral Therapy" for this type of problem. He believes that people who find it hard to act in their own best, long-term interest are rarely happy. But they are not truly "ill." While the quality of their life may be lower than they'd like, they don't really need psychiatrists. Wood maintains that many who live half-heartedly, who shrink from full involvement in life, are sometimes loath to improve their situations. Even though they suffer, they don't really want to change.

> At certain times . . . all of us are weak and indecisive. We become difficult to live with and blame others for our predicament. Feeling unloved, we become unlovable, and a vicious circle is set up. . . . When such individuals become aware that they are going to be asked to do things which, inevitably, they will find difficult—to undertake hard work, to give up many unprofitable pleasures and to lead a strict moral life as dictated by their consciences—they may shrink from the situation and return to more comforting but less helpful philosophies . . . (Wood, 1986, p. 20–21)

Elegant choice is a life-discipline—a way of staying mindful to what we are, to what we need and want, to what we're actually doing. However, since everyone is unique, each ultimately must define his or her own standard of what is and isn't "elegant." Each must find his or her own way. Fortunately, as we grow toward wholeness, the desire to take exactly this responsible route grows too. More fortunate still, there are a cluster of consistent values inherent in the elegant choice.

The elegant choice expresses the Being values: those universally-held sacred values we could call "the Good," for short. For most, making choices that embody such values takes a degree of effort and will. Thus, demonstrating the Being values in our life develops our will and our goodness simultaneously. This fact itself contributes to our healing. "Purity of heart," wrote Kierkegaard, "is to will one thing."

> Only the Good is one thing in its essence and the same thing in each of its expressions. Take love as an illustration

. . . the one who truly loves . . . loves with all of his love. It is wholly present in each of his expressions. He continues to give it away as a whole, yet he keeps it intact as a whole, in his heart. Wonderful riches! When the miser has gathered all the world's gold in his sordidness—then he has become poor. When the lover gives away his whole love, he keeps it entire—in the purity of his heart. (Kierkegaard, 1938, p. 60)

In other words, our choice changes us—in the direction of the quality and nature of the choice. There is no way out. For good or bad, we are defined and molded by our choices. Since only the Good is whole enough to be one thing in all its expressions, by choosing elegantly (i.e., the Good) we become like that thing. The Good, through our choice, touches, enters, develops, and transforms us.

Shall a man will one thing, then this one thing that he wills must remain unalterable in all its changes, so that by willing it he wins immutability. (Kierkegaard, 1938, p. 60)

Willing one thing is elegant. By willing the elegant choice—which is always, as I am striving to show, the Good in all its infinite expressions—we become immutable, whole, one thing, complete.

DEVELOPING OUR GOOD WILL

I promised I'd be practical. Concretely, even mundanely, here is how this method works in everyday matters. A friend was grossly overweight. She'd tried dieting and had lost weight—and gained it back. Lost, gained, lost, gained. Finally, to herself she said firmly, "I'm going to stop thinking in terms of a final goal. I'm just going to handle the *process* of the way I eat, eat more healthfully, eat less, pay attention to how I conduct myself during a meal, pay more mind to the way I prepare it and consume it, meal by meal, day by day." She lost about fifty pounds. To this day she is still losing weight, and it's as if a new person is coming into being. Her new-found self-respect gives her more control. So does her sense that she—her deeper person—can manage her life. As she said, "If I can do this, I can do anything."

This woman willed *one* thing: to be healthy. This was, for her, the Good—something more elegant, both in motive and process, than dieting per se. From the point of that one choice, a trajectory of other choices—and self-improvement—was put into place. Everything in her life has been touched by this steady and gradual improvement. It is not only a more slender, aesthetic body that benefits my friend's life, although that helps her overall health and energy. Rather her choice itself liberates her from a lifetime battle with food because she willed the Good.

Returning momentarily to Garth Wood's framework for such topics, one of the tenets of Moral Therapy is that we always need to do what our conscience—the part-that-knows—tells us what we ought to do, even though we don't *feel* like doing it (Wood, 1986).

For example, as my friend enabled herself to choose her good, she empowered herself. Her conscience told her to get healthier. As soon as she chose in line with this directive, she achieved her secondary goal of looking prettier. When we select what is in line with our Good, our true self-interest, we are able to will more such choices for our good (and that of others)—a veritable synergy of benefits.

Elegant choice always develops our good. In the long run this heals us interiorly. Usually we are unaware of the power inherent in our own will, unconscious of the consequences of each tiny act. The Zen Buddhists, like the western world's saints, have understood the need for immaculate attention to detail. Above all, the staying-power and cleansing properties of disciplined attention help us develop our good will. As we are able to stay centered on the present, as we focus ourselves in all purity and with full attention on the now-moment, we can *see* that one thing is better than another. Knowing and doing are related, and the more aware we are of what we do, the more capable we are of taking the elegant direction. This is what brings people to enlightenment, transforming them into Zen Masters. The practice, if there is one, is sublimely simple. At the same time, it is demanding work.

To put such matters into a predigested plan or recipe format would trivialize the discussion and sever us from the very concentration needed for the work. However, several principles suggest themselves at the outset. The first principle is that of developing our "good will."

Good will means we are able to choose, and desire to choose, that which is good, and that we *enjoy* exercising our will in this direction. Elegant choice requires that we have understanding of what we truly value and hold in high esteem. It isn't enough just to promote a sort of Victorian discipline by which we force ourselves into preconceived, idealized, boxes of behavior. In my discussion about right livelihood (Sinetar, 1987), I've explored at least a few ways in which we can determine what is more important to us. Basically, we educate our will to help us grow.

Shortly after his conversion to Catholic Christianity, St. Augustine began a treatise entitled *On Free Choice of the Will*, in which he stressed that the only difference between the happy and the unhappy is that happy persons love their own good will. They enjoy doing what is good and what is good for them. As we attempt to raise the level of our simplest action, we must keep this in mind. We help ourselves grow if we ask ourselves frequently—and especially as we get ready to choose poorly—whether or not we love our own good will.

Ironically, centuries later, when Maslow described the self-actualizing person, he wrote that the signs of self-betrayal (i.e., bad, unhealthy, unproductive, self-defeating choices) were almost nil. It was these persons in whom the giving up of "lower" desires (e.g., addictions, toxic relationships, unattractive habits, etc.) was natural. In these persons the desire for "higher" pleasures (e.g., duty, sustained effort, creative endeavor, mature, brotherly, compassionate love, etc.) was natural. In other words, those who grow toward full selfhood simultaneously grow to love their own good will. Duty and pleasure become one and the same: the gap between "work" and "play" is closed. Our will to choose the good grows as we do.

Sometimes we receive a payoff for keeping an unproductive habit in place. We must root this payoff, this supposed benefit, out of our unconscious and deal with it honestly. For example, in our sexually-oriented society women have traditionally been expected to be slim and attractive. In this way they remain valued sex-objects for men's approval and pleasure. Many strong-minded independent women (unconsciously or not) prefer to stay heavy. Better to be plumpish than treated as an objet d'art. At least, by keeping some extra padding of fat on their frames, they maintain a measure of control over their destiny. Such control can be manifested in a sense of increased self-definition ("I'll decide what my body is going to look like, not men, the media, my parents, society"). Fatness may stave off unwanted attention, relationships, and submission to the standards of others. Before such women can become slim, they must understand why they have chosen to be heavy.

The outcomes of our choices may be self-defeating on the surface, yet can also be dependable ways for gaining a measure of freedom from other irritations. The heavy woman may set herself free from unwanted sexual attention or involvements. The uncommitted or irresponsible person can thereby avoid requests or dependencies of others, have more time for personal interests or recreational persuits. If each of us is honest about our unhelpful choices, we see that most of them are relatively easy to change. Of this, St. Augustine comments:

> . . . if we should love and embrace with our will the good will and place it before all other things . . . then those virtues as reason demonstrates, will dwell in our spirit, and to possess them [i.e., virtues] is to live rightly and honorably. From this it is established that whoever wants to live rightly and honorably, if his will for this surpasses his will for [the unhelpful thing] achieves this good so easily that to have what he wills is nothing other than the act of willing. (Ibid., p. 28)

When my friend realized the value of losing weight once and for all, when she willed to change her direction, she ended up realizing, "If I do this, I can do anything." She learned she could "do anything," because her desire for the elegant was stronger than her food-cravings. As noted previously, her willing of the good strengthened her good will overall—in other words, she willed to develop herself as a human being and that will manifested in every other conceivable area of her life. The weight "solution" was simply useful as an instrument, a vehicle, for developing her good will.

DEVELOPING OUR CONCENTRATION

A second principle in choosing elegantly could be called the "principle of developed concentration." This can be stated as follows: to the extent we stay mindful—concentrated on the present moment—to that extent we can monitor or control our choices so that they are beneficial to our long-term interests. Our developed focus keeps us in touch with what we're doing, as opposed to our acting largely through unconscious habits and drives. And when we possess a mindful presence we stay in touch with every aspect of ourselves: our thought processes, attitudes, behaviors, preferences and (and this is key to the development of our good will) our foibles. Even the consequences of small actions and thought show themselves to us when we stay focused.

Fritz Perls, father of Gestalt Therapy, believed that increased concentrative powers had therapeutic benefit. He, perhaps more than anyone else, was able to link the entire person—the whole or Gestalt expressions of the person—to subtle, though varied patterns of mind-bits, habits and avoidances. Again and again he recommended mental disciplines for building up and strengthening the muscles of concentration. These muscles are a prime requisite if we would notice our resistances, distractive tendencies, mental incoherencies, repressed bits of what Perls calls "messy thinking." One technique he advocated was that of listening to music. Sounding more like a Zen Master, Perls valued the inner silence that could, ultimately, let one "see" one's own distraught and unruly character:

> Nowhere else [other than listening to music] can you check up on your powers of concentration. In full concentration there is no room for both listening to music and thinking and dreaming. . . . Perhaps the most valuable outcome of the training in internal silence is the achievement of a state beyond evaluation (beyond good and bad) . . . (Perls, 1969, p. 215)

In sum, by enabling ourselves to choose the good, by learning what we value, by staying awake to the ways in which we stand in our own way, we also teach ourselves something about the kind of person we truly are. We can watch ourselves trying to express our best self, yet often unable to. To express our good, the highest standard within us, means we must hold to what is difficult. As the poet Rainer Maria Rilke advises, we must love what is difficult. We must love the will in us that chooses the Good, and simultaneously develop the imaginative strength to create pleasingly superior images to serve as the *blueprint* for our good will.

Holding to what is difficult is—forgive me, Rainer—so very difficult. That's why we don't do it. We avoid it like the plague, orienting ourselves toward the easy. Yet almost anyone can hold on. Many people do. We can do it slowly, with the most minute and gradual of steps, first thinking about what it is we value and then moving toward that in spirit and attitude. Bit by bit, we move toward our good by choosing it. In the process, we transform ourselves, changing for the better every time we choose, in direct proportion to the quality of our choice. Elegant choice helps us raise the quality of our lives.

2

The Value of Self-Definition

Probably a crab would be filled with a sense of personal outrage if it could hear us class it without ado or apology as a crustacean, and thus dispose of it. 'I am no such thing,' it would say; 'I am *myself, myself* alone.'

> William James,
> *Varieties of Religious Experience*

Not long ago, I gleefully read about five teenagers who achieved perfect scores on their SAT exams. It cheered me considerably to learn that these five were each crisply unique, self-styled persons who had a flair for being themselves. One young man had strong opinions on just about everything. He thought his school's honor society represented the "antithesis of all that is good and noble in humanity. The people whom they think of as leaders are skilled at bootlicking and being sheepish." About sports, he was equally bold: "The voyeurism in spectator sports is disgusting and counter-productive. The audience is essentially brain dead." (*People*, June 1987)

Another youth, also a perfect-scorer, wouldn't tell his friends about his test achievement, feeling it would be bragging. And a third—photographed wearing his father's Army jacket and sneakers decorated with palm trees—stayed out of an honors program in order to take an international cooking class. Of his scholastic accomplishments (he has a 5.2 grade point average on a scale that uses 4.0 as the equivalent of an A average) he says, "I didn't take the SAT all that seriously. It just proves that if you're not competitive, you'll do better." (Ibid)

When I shared this article with business friends, many thought it irritating. One business colleague called the boys "adolescent," adding, "They're fighting the system. That's what one does at thirteen." His words gave me pause, and I asked him to elaborate. Seems he too had tried to buck convention when he was younger, and had a college professor who'd told him rebelling was wrong, unproductive, immature. "It's not what you're against that counts," my friend was taught, "but what you're for that matters. What are you for?" And, in his teens, my friend couldn't answer since he didn't really know yet. An unfair question for a youngster, I think it's a fair and a good one for adults.

POSITIVE REBELLION

Reviewing my own happy response to the article, I realize I love self-definition however and wherever I encounter it. Perhaps this is the type of positive rebellion that all self-definition requires, the knowledge of what we stand for and, yes, even what we're against. Truly, it takes Herculean effort to know oneself, define oneself (first, for oneself, and then for others) and then to live out that knowledge, boldly or quietly in our own self-styled way. Doing so can take a long time, even a life-time.

This is more a struggle for some than for others. Some people have a restless energy, even in childhood. This is a dynamic force that can assert itself all through their life. If we relate to this, then we may find ourselves always striving for achievement. We might be attention-getters. We may "act out" to use an educator's term, despite our best and deeper intention

to behave properly. When I was about fourteen I overheard
two of my favorite teachers discussing me. Unaware that I was
nearby, they complained that it was difficult to have me in
class: I daydreamed too much, I laughed and fooled around, I
didn't take my studies seriously. Worse, they said I influenced
the others to behave as I did. I was stunned. I had not known
I'd been insensitive to their needs and wished they'd spoken to
me directly. (Perhaps they had, and I had not heeded.) After
that experience, I tried resolutely to contain my restlessness,
but I know I missed their mark.

Generally students are expected to be seen and only heard
when they say whatever furthers a teacher's point of view. Of
course, the gifted, "born teacher" does not expect compliance
or passivity, but even gifted teachers find overly-energetic, expressive students disruptive at times.

Some people learn to be compliant early in their lives. If
their parents caution them against being seen or heard, against
being uniquely themselves, if such lessons are learned too painfully, it is commonsense that, as one option, they easily shut
down their self-defining mechanisms and try to blend in with
everyone else. Intimidated into conforming, they are punished
into a safe, invisible way of being that can last a lifetime.

Others learn these same lessons independently. Because
of inordinate sensitivities, their chosen, and at the time quite
prudent, path is to stay hidden. They may become introverted
or secretive about themselves. Sometimes it is just sensible to
keep our plans to ourselves of course. But while it is one thing
to control our self-disclosures so that the information we give
out works for us, it is quite another to have no option, to be
brutalized—by others or by our own hypersensitive response
mechanisms—into lifelessness. Thus, when thinking about
how our choices either free us toward self-expression or lock
us up inside our skins, it is helpful to survey the injunctions we
bring from childhood into adulthood. These rules tell us what

to think about self-definition: about the value of nonconformity, creativity and independent thinking.

CONFORMITY AS HABIT

When we are small, physically and emotionally dependent on adults who have power and authority over us, it pays to stay agreeable, conforming, "nice." Authority figures are sources of love and protection for us. Once we learn such habits of compliance, it's hard to break them. These interactive habits are often excellent strategies for getting what we need and want when small. They continue into adulthood when we no longer need or want to placate people. But we still act in docile ways because it *feels* comfortable—feels like the correct, successful thing to do.

One of my favorite authors, the now-deceased psychiatrist Robert Lindner, wrote about the value of positive rebellion. Lindner believed that for most of us there exists an Eleventh Commandment: an unwritten yet powerful law of society that demands that human persons conform, adjust, give in to the dictates of mass mind. But Lindner also taught that the instinct for rebellion is a most human characteristic, one which is at the heart of our very souls.

> . . . the efforts to snuff out the small flame of liberty that burns within all of us never cease. Wherever he turns in his frantic search for selfhood and individual expression, the growing child is met by the injunction to adjust. . . .

> Everywhere and at once, alone or among his fellows, each of us dreads individuality—and, at the same time, longs for it as a lover yearns after his love. To me this is the fundamental conflict of our time. (Lindner, 1952, p. 236)

To me, this is a fundamental human conflict for *all* time. Its most usual outlet is the battle between highly creative persons and society. Happily, not everyone submits to the injunction to adjust. Some fortunate persons are even encouraged from their earliest days—either by circumstances, or by their equally unusual, idiosyncratic parents—to follow their own distinctive call. Such individuals, when they grow up along wholesome, expressive, productive lines, usually become our most creative citizens.

The difference between the conforming child, however gifted and bright, and the nonconforming one can often mean, respectively, the difference between someone who becomes an unimaginative, passive adult, and someone who becomes one who boldly makes his or her mark on the world. We ask: Aren't strong I.Q.'s and all the advantages of a good family enough to equip a child to become a productive adult? The answer is no— not when early life-experiences, parental influences and social pressures squelch a person's imagination, interpretive skill and desire for individuation.

INDIVIDUALITY IN CHILDHOOD

Many, if not most, highly resourceful, creative persons come from homes with what I'd call "jagged edges": traumatic, ignored, overly-strict or overly-permissive situations. Some come from circumstances in which one parent dominated the whole household. Others with more stable upbringings traveled extensively. Whatever the childhood, creative, self-defining persons have had very stimulating, exciting backgrounds. Some had love, a close bond with at least one parent, and richly varied experiences, conversation and educational opportunities. Others had solitary, lonely young lives that necessitated self-sufficient problem solving. Whatever the background, it is certain to stimulate thinking, reflection and inner richness.

Victor and Mildred Goertzel, in their study of hundreds of eminent and creative adults, vividly document this point with case after case study. These authors reveal that the parents of the famous and creative are not what we could call "Norman Rockwell" normal. While in these homes family value systems generally promote lifelong learning—including hot, vigorous debates, substantive readings and social or cause-oriented involvement—the backgrounds of famous achievers also include opinionated, abusive, dominant or careless parents.

Highly opinionated parents, for example, tend to produce children who extend the parents' opinionated ways, even extend their exact opinions. Where parents are involved in humanitarian reform, for instance, children often grow up to express similar, if not identical, concerns. For example, Jane Addams—who grew up in a Quaker home where her father, a friend of Lincoln's, was an active supporter of the poor and of peace-related projects—never undertook a cause that her father disapproved of.

Families in which the father was failure-prone typified at least half of the life-circumstances in the Goertzels' study. From daydreamer-fathers to impetuous, grandiose types (both types live easily without certainty, as do creative people in general), we find highly creative sons and daughters. George Gershwin's father was well-known for his business failures; the Gershwin family moved more than twenty times to different apartments, following their father's various business involvements. Freud was clearly his mother's son, and was reputed to hold his father in "mild contempt." William Carnegie, the father of Andrew, lost both means and livelihood when technological advances in the textile industries replaced hand-loom weavers in Scotland. At best, he was a marginal breadwinner, a dreamer, a gentle, unambitious man who married a strong, powerful woman. Had it not been for Margaret, Andrew's capable mother, who was able to plan and actually bring the whole family to America, the Carnegies might have gone hungry and perished. Carnegie's family profile—the failure prone father and the strong, dominating mother—characterizes the childhood of many famous, creative figures. *Ninety percent* of the dominating mothers in the Goertzels' study had failure-prone or weak husbands!

> The tendency to dominate is not racial, national or cultural. Wealthy mothers and poor mothers apply their will with identical intensity. The child who is talented in musical performance is the most vulnerable since his talent is evidenced early. (Goertzel, 1962, p. 87)

The parents of Yehudi Menuhin, Pablo Casals, Noel Coward and Giacomo Puccini—to name but a few—fall into the strong mother/weak (or nonexistent) father syndrome. In Frank Lloyd Wright's case, his mother's influence was felt even more keenly: this mother planned her son's career even before he was born, believing strongly in prenatal influence. She was determined that her son would be an architect, and while she was pregnant hung architectural wood carvings in the room that was to be his nursery. She was also certain that her unborn child would be a boy.

Families, fathers and especially mothers can also smother people into self-definition and creativity. For example, Clara Barton and Mary Baker Eddy were both smothered as children. So was General George Patton. Dominating parents and smotherers devote unusually concentrated attention to their children. Even when this suffocates the child initially, it is often the very irritant against which the child must fight to survive as an independent being. While developing the will and the wherewithal to solve their family predicament, such children find creative strategies and a toughness that last them a lifetime.

This was the case for the heroine of Andrea Dworkin's novel, *Ice and Fire*, who vowed what she would *not* tolerate as a grown-up. While still a little girl, the young heroine noticed a double-standard of conduct, freedoms and opportunity: one standard for the boys; one standard for her. She had a failure-prone father, an invalid mother, and these—coupled with the societal pressures of being a girl—gave her unique insight into what she was and what she was not:

> I had a cowgirl suit, a cowgirl hat, a gun, a holster. There was nothing more important than being a cowboy, even though I had to be a cowgirl because I had to wear a skirt. . . . But it was the gun I loved, and Annie Oakley. She wore a skirt, and was a crack shot and once we went to see her at a live show with Gene Autry. I wanted to be her or Roy Rogers or the Lone Ranger, not Dale Evans, not ever, not as long as I lived. (Dworkin, 1986, p. 13)

For the most part, mothers of highly creative youngsters want their children involved with ideas. They want them to be around stimulating playmates who are not easily bored. Money, influence and social status mean less to them than knowledge, cultural pursuits and lofty, finely honed value systems. These women are open to experience, to their feelings and their own interior life. They enjoy and seek out all varieties of people and cultural offerings. They encourage—they may demand—such openness in their young. Mothers who are also dominating, strong-willed or smothering will usually go to bat for their youngsters at school, defending them at all costs, as did the mothers of Edison and Einstein, against teachers who think them dull-witted or troublesome.

Thankfully, my own mother was this way. She encouraged, even insisted upon, my reading good books. She promoted our family's interests in every sort of cultural pursuit. She approved of, and supported, my involvement in any activity that attracted my attention such as drawing, ballet or horsebackriding. She herself has marvelous originality and no tolerance whatsoever for intrusions into her privacy.

When I was about eight, attending parochial school in the east, my mother was summoned to the school because I had refused to recite a prayer in class. Looking back, I believe I felt it somehow against my rights to be asked to do, in public, anything so private as pray. I'm not sure where I got this notion, since no one had ever taught it to me. But that idea was as much mine as my name. The nuns had given me a choice: either accept a spanking in assembly (or some such public humiliation) and *then* do the public prayer. Or, go home. I chose to go home—indeed that seemed a luxury.

Upon hearing the problem, my mother instantly withdrew me from the school. As we walked home that morning—and I remember this vividly: it was bright, sunny and bitingly cold; my mother had me by the hand and was talking to me very seriously—she apologized to me for having enrolled me there in the first place. She and I have had many disagreements, and not a few lasting scars and long silences have resulted from these. But I shall never forget my mother's example and influence in this area of my life: it was she who reinforced my innate sense that I have a right to feel what I feel and be what I am.

By contrast, the mothers of bright, solid but highly conforming children value compliance, and clean, mannerly friends for their offspring. For themselves, these women want money and prospering husbands with good professional connections. Ideas, culture, books do not interest them except as these are in vogue. Given a choice, these mothers prefer that their children make good grades, become competitive academically, and enter secure, well-paying professions as adults. Not surprisingly, even the very gifted young from these homes grow up to be flat, unimaginative, often overcontrolled adults.

Then too, researchers have found that teachers tend to prefer students with high I.Q.'s but low creativity—students who are agreeable, obedient and self-controlled. Creativity expert Paul Torrance has written that highly creative elementary school children often play when they should be doing schoolwork. To make matters worse for themselves, they enjoy learning so much (and here I distinguish between learning and schoolwork) that they seem to their teachers to be playing rather than studying. Also, as children they are hard to discipline, as, in adulthood, they are hard to manage as employees. (Sinetar, 1985)

INDIVIDUALITY IN ADULTHOOD

Self-actualizing adults are by definition highly individuated, creative persons. The effortless, spontaneous freedom from clichés and stereotypical behavior that marks the whole person is developed along with self-definition. These traits—spontaneity, conscious disregard or obliviousness to clichés or group norms—are natural by-products of the process of coming into one's own as a person. As people grow into the knowledge and doing of what they find most meaningful in life—how they like to live and to work, what their values are, the kinds of friends and relationships they want—they quite easily are able to talk about these things, act them out and demonstrate their values and inclinations in daily life.

While the potential for self-knowledge is inherent in all of us, we have seen how these sensitivities can get buried deep within, especially as we are often bullied and pressured as children to adopt a persona, a mask, that others find satisfactory and helpful to their objectives.

By contrast, the creative person—whose parents, early life-circumstances or strong actual desires encouraged openness—is the one whose self-trust spawns further distinctiveness when fully grown. Such a child grows up to be unafraid of his or her own insight, feelings and impulses. The person has greater self-acceptance for the idiosyncrasies of his own way of being. Alas, the majority of upstanding and "well-adjusted" adults have cut off much of what is best in them, as well as extinguishing the sense to select whatever will develop their own good. Whether it is a choice of reading material, spiritual direction or psychological assistance, such persons all too often choose what others tell them to choose or what they *think* others want them to pick.

On the other hand, and central to the explorations of this book, self-actualizing people are more efficiently developed in the areas of creativity and life-choices. They waste little time defending themselves against their own inclinations and ambitions, and they have less fear and are more self-accepting than average. Of this phenomenon, Maslow wrote:

> The normal adjustment of the average, common-sense, well adjusted man implies a continued successful rejection of much of the depths of human nature. . . . To adjust well to the world of reality means a splitting of the person. It means that the person turns his back on much in himself because it is dangerous . . . by doing so he loses a great deal too, for these depths are also the source of all his joys, his ability to play, to love, to laugh, and, most important for us, to be creative. By protecting himself against the hell within himself, he also cuts him off from the heaven within. (Maslow, 1962, p. 133-134)

Average, well-adjusted adults may know, at some level, that they have turned against themselves. Something within strains to emerge. Yet not knowing how to handle this, not finding much encouragement from spouses, peer group or family, they quiet their best emotions and impulses. They may heed the voice or example of stronger people or, perhaps just as likely, visit some expert (e.g., doctor, author, guru or another sort of tribal chief) who kindly, but skillfully, voices the most conservative concerns they have. It is the rare person, who can accept, without self-rebuke, the length of time it takes to find the way back to that natural joy, playfulness and originality that constitutes full personhood.

LOOKING WITHIN FOR ANSWERS

Often bright, capable, well-educated people write to me for advice. On one hand, they recognize part of themselves in the descriptions of actualizing people I have interviewed and written about. This allows them, some for the first time in their lives, to feel more at home with the alien, unknown part of themselves that they have strangled and cut off from outward expressions. But unaccustomed to thinking things through for themselves and all too practiced in seeking help from people with "authority," they again ask for direction.

Aspiring writers write for help getting started with a book. Men hoping to free themselves from spirit-breaking work write inquiring how to go about doing so. People who yearn to delve deeper into their own spirituality write asking "how" it is to be done. It is as if, to them, the expert, the authority, gives legitimacy and structure to their experience. Yet it is *we ourselves who must legitimize and structure our experience, even as we pull in ideas, images and input from external sources.*

This most personal work of defining ourselves is so subtle and delicate that no one else can do the self-creative work for us. Even to ask another puts us at risk: another might answer and thus interrupt the softness, the malleability of our yet-to-be-born, most tender self. We can ask the experts for input, but must look only to ourselves for answers.

Many are simply too receptive to the expert, the authority figure—as if they themselves were a clay-like entity upon which the more dominant person should imprint. In fact, it is entirely the other way around. *We* must imprint and mold the outer world to suit ourselves. We must create or structure events to our needs and to our liking, not in some horrible Machiavellian way but so as to be able to use ourselves meaningfully and productively. Wasn't this precisely what Jesus Christ taught by example as he healed the sick, raised the dead and turned water into wine? He was the Great Definer.

Yet most of us continue to look to others for advice and definition. A letter came to me from a woman long convinced she was a misfit. She experienced strong spiritual leanings within and consulted a psychiatrist about this. He confirmed her suspicion that something was amiss. But, upon reading my book, she was encouraged to learn that I, another professional, pronounced spirituality as "healthy":

> . . . it is your professional world which has always given me a scary sense that 'my reality' was not 'real reality.' I remember vividly that a very good psychiatrist told me that 'mystical experience' was simply the flip side of schizophrenia in that we hear voices . . . see things, etc. . . .

> Your book has finally given me a logical and (thank God) professional definition of myself and has undergirded a sense of confidence that I have always felt (in God), but have not felt in myself because I've not had a sense of belonging, feeling like I was outside of things . . .

We must beware any "professional definition" of ourselves. True, it is comforting to see ourselves described as "healthy" by someone we think of as knowledgeable, perhaps someone we respect, especially when that description is either flattering or full of optimism about our potential. This definition can help us feel as if we fit in somewhere, in a respectable category or box of some sort. Yet, herein lies the rub: there are always professionals who would assume definitional authority over us (perhaps I should say there are always any number of *people* who would assume definitional authority over us) and so—crave though we might the comfort of fitting into one of their snug definitional cubicles—we do better reserving all self-definitional rights to ourselves. For whoever defines us controls us by that very definition and we must be ever alert to the ramifications of their perceptions.

Our "self" is not something we find in the determinations, judgments or descriptions of another. Our self is an essential being—inside us, inside our skins, a core being, to be experienced, nurtured, known and loved (even created—in a way—outwardly) so that self can vigorously express itself in the world. In his lectures and writings psychiatrist Thomas Szasz points out that all authority controls when, and to the extent, it defines. In law, psychiatry and medicine, in all of the soft, "helping professions" such as social service work, and even in education, those in charge make infants of us by languaging us into categories that further their own objectives and professional interests.

> The struggle for definition is veritably the struggle to life itself. . . . In ordinary life, the struggle is not for guns but for words: whoever first defines the situation is the victor; his adversary, the victim. For example, in the family, husband and wife, mother and child do not get along; who defines whom as troublesome and mentally sick? . . . In

short, he who seizes the word imposes reality on the other: he who defines thus dominates and lives; and he who is defined is subjugated . . . (Szasz, 1974, p. 25)

Even this attempt to discuss the actualization process is an attempt to impose my reality construct on others. Still, and at the very least, with this logic and language I offer (and receive) hope: if we choose to adopt this paradigm, we thereby choose to liberate ourselves from further boxes.

Liberation is possible because these ideas help us *out* of externally imposed categories and classifications. The greater our resistance to being stereotyped and defined by others, the greater our chances for recovering a pure, clear sense of who we are as persons. And this is a first, exquisitely significant, step to our healing. For this pure, clear sense of self, has regenerative power, holds life within itself. This leads us, eventually, to completion.

3

Inscrutable Wholeness

> I am aware of something in myself whose shine is my reason. I see clearly that something is there, but what it is I cannot understand. But it seems to me that, if I could grasp it, I should know all truth.
>
> Anonymous. *Choice Is Always Ours*

A lovely example of self-definition, as it relates to ordinary, everyday life, comes in the spritely form and character of author Laurie Colwin's *Holly*. Holly is the cheery, competent and self-possessed heroine in Colwin's book, *Happy All the Time*. She is the beloved of another likeable soul, Guido, a young man who pines day and night for the girl. Guido's greatest wish is simply to touch Holly's hand. Then, miraculously, one night he gets invited to her apartment, and finds the place as splendidly distinctive as she is.

The apartment is white, airy and fresh-smelling. It is full of well-placed artifacts and artfully arranged objects. The bed is wrinkle-free, and has "hospital-corners"—an army sergeant's delight. Everything smells of lavender. Guido is, from that visit on, hopelessly in love.

> Everything seemed uncommonly rich to him: the print on the sheets, the pattern on the quilt, Holly's gleaming hair and earrings. . . . She was an only child, an only grandchild, and she was nearly perfect. She had her own ways,

> Holly did. She decanted everything into glass, and her long kitchen shelves were row upon row of jars containing soap, pencils, cookies, salt, tea, paper clips and dried beans. She could tell if one of her arrangements was off by so much as a sixteenth of an inch and she corrected it . . . (Colwin, 1978, p. 10)

Holly is distinctive, unique, all-of-a-piece. She is complete and perfect in her outward expression, and this matches what she senses herself to be inwardly. Paradoxically, while Holly is knowable there is a part of her that she values enough to keep to herself—an inscrutable side. Holly is strongly herself in all that she is, says and does, yet self-contained enough not to spill-all. It is not her outward traits, such as neatness or aesthetic perfectionism, that make her complete and distinctive. Rather, Holly *expresses* what she is. She has the audacity to define herself by herself.

In every obvious way, Holly translates herself into life, while hidden nonetheless. For the rest of his life, Guido loves Holly, but never fully knows her. Both her obvious eccentricities and what Guido cannot fathom fill him forever with wonder. Unquestionably, his wonder, his predicament, is ours as well and teaches us about the intricacies of wholeness: while we grow ever more distinctive, and thus become known to ourselves and others, correspondingly, a mysterious wonderful presence is born within us—this spirit of life can never be known fully. This spirit, even if we are forewarned, overwhelms our feeling-life with its grandeur—such is the depth of its beauty, its inscrutable, impenetrable richness. By preserving and respecting our privacy, we increase our individuality. Holly serves as a good model for such self-protective devices since she overtly keeps a piece of herself to herself. But she is only one example of what it might mean to function as a distinctively whole person.

Another might be just as distinctively whole if he is casual, relaxed, even physically sloppy. There is no Right Way—no single outward way of being perfectly oneself. Whatever way we sense ourselves to be within—precise and structured, casual and irreverent, vulnerable or crusty and rough—if we enact these same traits (as we know they exist in us at our best) we too grow toward perfection, toward completion.

Must I add that humans are flawed and faulty? Do I need to say, just to be on the safe side and so that I'm not misunderstood, that what I mean by "perfection" is not the sanitary absence of faults or human feelings? Rather I mean "completeness," that way of being wherein we possess a natural, graceful synergy amongst all our psychological sub-selves and warring drives.

At the highest levels of human maturation, all conflicted inner traits, that entire range of mixed impulses and contradictory passions that each possesses, are fused and organized. While there exists intricacy, or richness, of what can only be called *living truth* to the person, no ill-fitting, unresolved parts remain. All is harmonious, even if rough-edged and gritty. Even so, even though one may know himself as cohesive and whole, he is also aware that within, if only in latent form, are all human traits—the entire spectrum resides within.

The healthy, fully-functioning person knows herself as both strong and vulnerable, as pure yet tarnished, simultaneously special and ordinary. The one who feigns flawlessness is a long way from wholeness.

In the person of J.D. Salinger's exquisite little character, Teddy, we read something of the sort of perceptual unity and human completion I am trying to describe. We meet these qualities in one very rumpled, unruly and disheveled little child.

Teddy is a young boy who, from the age of around six, realizes that everything is God. In a conversation describing this revelation, he says that even earlier, when he was only four years old, watching his infant sister drink milk, he saw God pouring God into God. Teddy astounds his parents and professorial gurus with his wisdom and his trips out of what he calls "the finite dimension." But in most ways he is just a little boy, if an endearing one.

However enlightened and complete Teddy is, he is not a neat, precise character like Holly. He is simply an ordinary, extraordinary human:

> He was wearing dirty, white ankle-sneakers, no socks, seersucker shorts that were both too long for him and at least a size too large in the seat, an overly laundered T-shirt that had a hole the size of a dime in the right shoulder, and an incongruously handsome, black alligator belt. He needed a haircut—especially at the nape of the neck—the worst way, as only a small boy . . . can need one. (Salinger, 1953, p. 167)

Teddy, in stark contract to the well-groomed, quirky Holly, looks a mess. Yet he—more so than Holly—is a fully enlightened being, with a clearer, more penetrating sense of reality than any of the adults around him, including his parents. Teddy is "complete," therefore, necessarily perfect.

As Teddy demonstrates, the issue, finally, repeatedly, boils down to our *being* what we are, without paying heed to the preferences or definitions of others, without vain aspirations for stainless personage. Our personage *may* be stainless, but *if* it is, it is through grace. To try to hide our flaws only keeps us stuck, self-conscious and narcissistically self-involved.

BEING OURSELVES

Self-definition precedes style, and always accompanies actualization. For countless highly evolved humans—but not, I think, for all—style is a meaningless word. Stylists impart a vivid "picture" of themselves through their self-expression. They use, as building blocks, the simplest, easiest route: they choose life-styles, cars, clothes and so on as symbolic *and* actual vehicles to help others know who they are and what they value.

One friend found his former way of living too complicated. Upon realizing this, he gave away his expensive suits and furnishings just to liberate himself from time-consuming activities and possessions. In social situations he now presents himself more like Teddy—that is, he wears rumpled T-shirts, jeans and sneakers. Another friend moved toward greater formality and sophistication. Self-definition is *not* stylishness. But wholeness means being distinctive, even if we are distinctively ordinary.

To say who we are, even to ourselves, first means we must progressively develop a crisp sense of our own potentials and boundaries, that we pinpoint our cherished values as well as those rules, customs and beliefs that mean nothing to us. This entails not so much a "right-wrong" moral stance as it does a simple recognition, over time, of who and what we are. We must decide how we want to invest our energies and conduct our lives. Only then can life take on fresh meaning and express our most personally relevant purposes.

In this regard, we may find we must initially learn to defend ourselves against those who judge us wrong for the way we are and choose to live. Sometimes our failure to spontaneously or energetically do battle against the domination, manipulation or really hurtful responses of others means we must do much psychological homework before we can live our own unique life. As we risk exposing our core self to others, we also risk others intruding upon what we have revealed. This risk-taking takes skill.

Can we, for example, speak up for ourselves when someone important to us disagrees with us, criticizes us or tells us how we "ought" to be? If we are silent in such instances, can we nevertheless keep firm hold on ourselves, remain centered? Are we tenacious in executing plans that matter, despite the obstacles in our path or the expectations of others? At the same time do we retain the power to change directions at a moment's notice, without undue explanation or justification? Can we act upon our finer impulses, such as expressing compassion for someone or showing politeness in some awkward social situation, in the face of contrary, opposite behaviors from others? Can we, in other words, go against the crowd in order to bring forth our most tender sensibilities when friends or family think us silly or naive for our sentiments? Do we laugh along with others at racial or ethnic slurs, in order to be agreeable, or laugh with them even at ourselves when our best instincts are the butt of a joke?

THE PRIVACY FACTOR

Do we "tell all" in the guise of trying to be completely open, and thus set ourselves up for attack—pave the way with our own masochism for unsolicited, unwanted advice about our decisions and choices? There are so many ways we undo ourselves when unsure about what we're about. A man of forty, who works near my home as a caretaker, is actually a fine nature photographer. For a few years now he has quietly worked at his caretaking job to earn enough money so that he can grow in experience and skill as a photographer. Recently he quit his job to devote his undivided attention to photography. At the same time he felt ambivalent about whether or not he would return to a regular job after a few months. His friends and neighbors kept inquiring about his plans, and he—in the hope of being fully disclosing—told them his truth: that he didn't know what he was going to do, that he only wanted a few months off, that he was looking for answers. This opened him up to their editorial and quite parental suggestions for his life. Finally, he realized that he didn't need to tell all.

> Now when people ask me what I'm doing, I put my answer into words that give me a little privacy. I give them something to work on with my reply, like saying that I'm retiring early; that I'm going to concentrate on photography; that I'm working on a deal to open up my own business. When I'm confident, I do this easily. When I'm at a low ebb and want approval, my answer somehow prompts their advice and criticisms. It is as if I put them in a parent's role and myself in the child's place just to satisfy their curiosity and my insecurity.

Psychiatrist Natalie Shainess frames such tendencies in terms of women's suffering. But I sense that "self set-up" is a *human* failing, a genderless problem which occurs most usually when we lack positive assertion skills or want to hear that our actions are in keeping with the wishes and expectations of others. Self set-ups are a covert tool for procuring strokes, for closing-up ambiguous, awkward spaces in conversation or for translating inner discomfort into conversational outlets. Of this pattern, Shainess perceptively writes,

> When masochistic people feel defensive about something, which is most of the time, they invariably attempt to correct it, to fix it up. Just as invariably, that attempt makes things worse. They feed the flames rather than putting them out. Learning not to do that involves learning to say no to themselves: No, I will not rush to explain, to rectify, to mollify, to disarm . . . I will keep still. (Shainess, 1984, p. 68)

Self-defining persons master the knack of knowing *when* to keep still and when to talk about their plans or problems. They creatively choose—quite elegantly—to transmit just enough information so that ultimately their verbal patterns serve them, support their plans and needs, act as a life-enhancing vehicle rather than a self-defeating one. They are innocently shrewd.

Indeed there is a connection between the passion to do something and the self-protective strategies we devise to see our efforts through to completion. Certainly we can appreciate the kind of borderline self-flagellation that exists when we expose our ideas too soon, talk about our plans too often, or volunteer too freely, give too much information about ourselves. When we find ourselves quizzed by someone about "why" we're doing something, it is helpful to go back to our *own* remarks preceding their why-question.

"Why?" means justify. If we are asked "Why?" too frequently, we can be sure that somewhere in the labyrinth of ourselves exists a self-defeating mechanism. We want the negative input. Part of the reason we solicit input and comment from others in the first place is to stop ourselves from acting boldly. When we're sure of ourselves, certain about what we want to do, no one dares to offer advice or ask us "Why?"

When we volunteer too much, or the wrong thing, or when (as did the reader quoted earlier) we express relief at finding someone else's "professional definition" of what we are, we undermine ourselves at the core. This predictable self-sabotage further splits and fragments us, prevents our recovering the bond-to-Self, thwarts our wholeness. To move toward wholeness we must learn to tolerate suspense while choosing in ways that build our trust and faith in ourselves.

LOVING OURSELVES

To love our own distinctiveness is to heal our inclination to self-sabotage. Love, if and when we choose it, severs the split within, gives us the strength and faith to pursue with intensity, passion and courage the things that give meaning and purpose to our lives. The quality of love I refer to has many faces yet remains unalterably itself throughout all its disguises. It gradually unifies and completes anything it touches. Beyond image, concept, theory and the material world, this love develops in us that consistent innate loyalty of spirit and heart that energizes our right choices, our correct communications and our self-possessed ability to wait patiently for life answers and direction.

This love also loves the other-as-self, rejoices in life, even in tiresome situations or in illness or pain. Love lets us be grateful for all things, for life itself. Love is pure, positive energy. It is full, concentrated focus and sustained effort. Sometimes compassionate and meek, at other times this love is uninhibited, unassailably fierce. Always life-sustaining, love is the fundamental backdrop against which, through which, all elegant choices are made.

A client of mine, a corporate attorney, married a dysfunctional woman, severely mentally ill. They have been married for decades. Again and again he rescues her, much as an alcoholic's spouse rescues his or her mate. He is there when she is abusive. He spends huge sums on the best psychiatrists. He sends their children to boarding schools when their mother becomes too ferocious and hateful to be safely around. Gradually, he realized he hurt himself (*and* hurt his wife and the children) by sustaining the existing framework of their marriage.

Believing in commitment, straining to keep his vows in-

tact, he remained long after he knew there was something seriously wrong. He loved her. He loved their life together when
she was well, but realized that whenever his wife was hospi-
talized, separated from him, her mental health improved.
Every time he reestablished intimacy and physical proximity,
she deteriorated.

"Is she," he wondered aloud to me, "capable of a loving
and normally intimate marriage relationship?" I could not answer. But the many psychiatrists he retained felt that her problem was a cry for help, perhaps a plea for solitude. As he sensed
that her unconscious wish was *not* to be married, when he admitted that he loved her enough to leave her, when he understood that he himself chose someone now incapable of mature,
wholesome love—someone who needed time alone in order to
heal—he left. When he understood he himself might not have
been a mature, wholesomely loving person, then he took his
first positive steps on behalf of his entire family and himself.
He talked openly with his wife about his own discoveries, and
she—not surprisingly—agreed. She seemed relieved to have
found an answer. At this time they are separated, although still
married, still working on their respective selves. They live in
different homes yet are committed to each other, and have
greater intimacy and trust than before. The children live with
their father: for the first time in their lives, they have a stable
and predictable home life. What seems, on the surface, to be
an unloving act might not be. Things are not always what they
seem. Only we can know what they are. Only we can know
our motives behind our choices. In this family's case, a new
form of marriage may save the marriage. In this case, love separated a family.

My client's love—for himself and ultimately for his wife
and children—developed in the midst of his choosing the difficult, unappealing and unconventional step. By maturely
withdrawing himself from the form of conventional marriage,

he demonstrated keen understanding for his wife's continual aberrant behavior: that, as their psychiatrist has suggested, and who can say for sure, her dysfunction may represent her bid for time-alone, so as to sort out her dis-eased subjective self by herself. By choosing a fearful path, the one he previously fought against, my client demonstrated an empathic, generous love. Healing for the entire family came about with this choice. In time, he underscored this healing by forgiving himself for years of misguided choices.

SELF-FORGETFUL OBJECTIVITY

We must not think any book can tell us *what* we should do when it comes to life's tough issues. While for the majority a rule-of-thumb approach may be good advice, for us—as individuals, at a unique point in time, with circumstances that cannot be addressed by rule-of-thumb principles—*form* cannot infallibly direct us. If we try to obey iron-clad rules over the course of our life, we too easily become persons who are true to the letter of the law but who kill the *spirit* of the law by their legalistic conduct. Rule and form *can* help: I do not suggest improvisation just for the sake of originality. But neither must we put the proverbial cart before the horse. Each choice is unquestionably dependent upon a host of variables. Only the individual knows where his or her virtue resides in a matter.

My client learned that by clinging to the form of marriage, his choices were borne of a lesser quality of love. Once he considered his wife's deepest needs, as well as his own and those of his children, he embodied a productive, strengthened love. Finally he was able to nourish the emotional starvation in his marriage in a potent manner. Yet, to do this, he had to contradict rules of conduct he learned as a young man.

Thomas Merton wrote often, always eloquently, of the in-

herent problem in following formulas. He admitted that the
most basic question we can ask is "What must I do?" Yet, as
basic a question as this is in life's difficult regions, there is no
easy answer. We must first think things through for ourselves.
This means we listen to that "still small voice" within so as to
cut through the unrealistic ideals we may be trying to live by.
Merton, ever the helpful teacher, thought it essential that our
ideals, however theologically praiseworthy, be synchronized
with reality:

> Ideals, which are generally based on universal aesthetic
> norms 'for everybody'—or at least for those who are 'seek-
> ing perfection'—cannot be realized in the same way in each
> individual. Each one becomes perfect, not by realizing one
> uniform standard of universal perfection in his own life,
> but by responding to the call and love of God, addressed
> to him within the limitations and circumstances of his own
> peculiar vocation. (Merton, 1964, p. 29)

Self-definition means thinking of ourselves and of our
lives in a deeply responsive, subjective manner—not simply
positioning ourselves as an attractive object for others to ad-
mire. Even if we prefer thinking of ourselves and life through
a vantage point of art (which many philosophers and especially
Oriental writers would have us do) we must unify our inner
and outer expressions to any number of varied influences.

In a life-as-art approach we still must synergistically create one whole picture. The details of our life expressions, the
style and character of each life-stroke enhance the overall,
broad brushstroke image of what we are as persons. The details
of our life add up to be what we do and value, how we live and
work, what and how we choose—not only simple, daily matters, but also during the difficult times, in the context of real-
world circumstances. If we know how we function best, if we

assess our worldly effectiveness we can help ourselves choose elegantly.

This means we must identify what is important to us. It means we develop clear objectivity with which to "see" our circumstances, and those around us, *as they are:* not as we ideally wish them to be. It is, in the final analysis, through our objective awareness that we are able to productively merge the inner person we are with outer realities, bringing our visions and dreams to fruition in concrete ways. Loss of objectivity is the loss of definitional power. With that loss, others—family, close friends, society, professionals—or rules and institutional guidelines gain too great an influence on us. These become our gods. While others can mightily help us, with input or interpretive analysis of our situations, in the end only we understand our own experiential phenomenon. But to do so, we must merge our subjective life with outer realities. This is our responsibility as human beings.

By contrast, through wholesome, objective self-love, we more easily admit when we're at fault or weak. We know if we have distorted something so that we feel better or emotionally worse than necessary. The person who lacks objectivity is usually the one who fixes too much attention on herself. So does the one who exaggerates the outer circumstance so that others feel he has lost perspective and blown things out of proportion, made more of things than warranted. To think and act as if the whole world revolved around us, to believe that people are interested in our every reason for acting, is to inflate our importance. People simply don't need to know our rationalizations and justifications for every little thing. What's more, they don't usually care. To care too much about another's opinion, it seems, is just as harmful as to care too little. In either case— by caring too much or too little—we lack a firm grip on reality. We can easily gain this back by being more objective. People who continually fail at work, who are frequently fired from jobs, for example, but who don't know why, are persons who lack objectivity. This lack prevents their best insights and decision-making.

A priest told me that his brother, when in his late teens, continually asked their mother for advice: "What shall I be when I grow up? What should I study in college?" With all sincerity, his mother answered "Son, no one cares what you do. I care, because I'm your mother. But don't worry too much about what I think either. Just choose what you can do well, what you enjoy, what you can give a lifetime of effort to. Then get on with it. Forget about yourself. Think what you can do to help others—from the source of your own special talents. That's all anyone cares about—what you give them of yourself from within yourself."

Yet there is a risk here. Once we live this way, once we forget ourselves, we live dangerously. Then we are separated from the world, live apart from its way of seeing us or doing things. I have already written extensively about those actualizing adults who spontaneously reinterpret life according to their own unique perceptions. They speak more vividly than I can about the rejections and social difficulties of this independent life-stance.

In his splendid little book, *St. Francis of Assisi*, G.K. Chesterton repeats this point, but through a frame of reference of the turmoils faced by young St. Francis. This odd, impulsive holy man struggled long and hard with the quirks he knew to be his own true self. He spoke to animals, to the sun, to the wind and moon. He was ridiculed constantly by his neighbors and friends.

As an example of this, before his conversion, Francis was rejected—physically thrown out—by his own father. Around this time in his life, in grief over this and other humiliations, he crawled into a cave of sorts. He stayed in there for an indistinct length of time, but was clearly thought to be a fool and a crazy one at that by his community. In that cave he experienced a life-shattering conversion and emerged a saint. After that however, St. Francis continued in his unique, ceremonial and often comic manner. This apparently was his way, his inscrutable brand of completion. No one understood him—not even the Church. Everything he did was dramatic, different, eccentric. He was his own person, in his own world, considered by others a lunatic, even if a lovable one. Were it not for his intense reverence for all life and for God, he would never have been taken seriously at all. However, fortunately for him and for us, he never took the world too seriously either:

> . . . he deliberately did not see the mob for the men. What distinguishes this very genuine democrat from any mere demogogue is that he never either deceived or was deceived by the illusions of mass-suggestion. Whatever his taste in monsters, he never saw before him a many-headed beast. He only saw the image of God multiplied . . . (Chesterton, 1957 ed., p. 96)

I bring St. Francis into this discussion about pulling away from conventionality, because if he had concentrated energy and attention on what people thought, the world would not have known him as a saint. Then he would most effectively have undermined his own power and his love of God. One could argue that St. Francis lacked objectivity. In the way we commonly mean the word—high rationality—this is true. Yet here was a detached and separated man, who ultimately loved God and God's creatures so much he completely forgot himself. To be objective, in the way I mean it here, is to live for the sake of others, to live effectively (even if strangely), to live responsibly so as to give more than we exploit, exhaust or oblige others. This St. Francis did with passion. Also, I most emphatically draw parallels between what psychologists term "wholeness" and what theologians call "saintly." St. Francis' degree of wholeness was immense. This achievement (if I might call a grace "accomplishment") flowed in part from his willingness to live apart from the world—trusting his own perceptions—although he flung himself into the world with abandon. Were it not for his letting go of his socially inspired "self," his transformed way of being could not have come about. He would have then too tenaciously clung to safe expressions, to the approval of others, to the selfish life. The principle behind these paragraphs is this: if we can transcend our social milieu, society in general, ourselves as we customarily have known our "self" to be, we can grow whole. Social-transcendence affords us the objectivity needed for effective functioning. In detachment we become strategic.

In the eyes of others, the whole person, the actualized person, is sometimes the strangest, most misunderstood misfit. Rightly so, for to be whole means to be an original being— unlike the herd in outward manifestations, although not necessarily unconventional in either dress, behavior or inner inclinations. Each of us is like others in some ways, yet also unique. The more whole we become, the more unafraid we are of being simply ourselves.

Wholeness also demands we live creatively—in a way that can make us seem to be what is politely called "a character." Now just because someone is a character does not mean he is whole. But it is certain the actualizing person protects her idiosyncrasies (especially the interior ones). Our tender sensibilities, which add up to be what or who we are, are often what we try to hide or deny.

In St. Francis' case, we see an extreme example of idiosyncrasy-in-action. He was indeed an odd man, even among saints. Chesterton describes his behavior in heart-rending terms, showing us along the way what it can mean when someone rids himself or herself of mechanical, robotic mannerisms and conduct:

> . . . the act is always unexpected and never inappropriate. Before the thing is said or done it cannot even be conjectured; but after it is said or done it is felt to be merely characteristic. It is surprisingly and yet inevitably individual. (Ibid., p. 84)

Therein lay part of Saint Francis' power—that he was fully and completely himself, without the self-conscious controls or narcissistic self-involvement that cripples most people. As we grow more integrated and individual there is every likelihood that we too will consider ourselves, and perhaps be considered by others, "odd." Holly, the fictional character discussed earlier, were she a real-life character, might be branded "perfectionistic" by psychologists, or as "anal-retentive," by fast-talking sophisticates. Teddy, Salinger's hero apparently has premonitions of his death, yet meets his fate willingly. What should we label that? And what of us? What do we think of our own core-self? What box have we accepted for ourselves? To be whole, we must choose in ways that let us live out our originality—no more, no less.

There are no assurances that what we choose to be or do will be considered "right" or attractive by other people. Moreover, we no doubt disrupt others through our choice-making when we are individual. This is yet another reason that preserving some privacy and our own counsel are helpful assists to growth. If we have privacy in some special areas of life, we limit unwanted advice. This is essential to our development. For example, as we become less self-conscious and more spontaneous, our commitments to a particular life plan *increase*. We become more passionately ourselves and so may alienate sig-

nificant others who are important to our lives. If we open ourselves to advice at every turn, we become unnecessarily
imposed upon by endless discussion about our decisions. The
person who decides to embark upon a different life-style, for
instance, or the one who changes career course in mid-stream,
or the one daring to live outside the traditional norms will want
a small amount—if not a lot—of privacy, at least in the planning stages of the altered course. Ironically, as we see in a later
chapter, the higher our self-esteem, self-knowledge and integrity (all traits of wholeness) the likelier it is we can know our
values, keep our word, stick to a life-course that meets *our* approval, become reliable in our love and work. This means the
unpopular choices we make in the earliest stages of growth may
easily evolve into quite solid, popular decisions—even amongst
former critics.

Nevertheless, even with these benefits, the choices born
of self-definition are not easy, not popular. It is ever so much
safer to simply fit in. One danger of self-defining acts, as mentioned, is that we upset others' plans and expectations as we
choose to live out our own life-truths. Another danger is, especially in the early stages of individuation, that we think too
much of ourselves, wasting valuable energy and time. The
tendency to be overly involved with ourselves renders us useless, since a no-win narcissism flows from all self-preoccupation. This seriously undermines our best intentions.

A third danger along this path is to think too *little* of our
own perceptions. I have already discussed this stumbling
block, but, in summing up, want to add a word more. When
we devalue our talents, when we discount our own inclinations, we also discard the best we have to offer others. Here,
too, we render ourselves useless. When we let others confuse
us or direct and control us, so that we don't become active directors of our own life-script, we thwart everyone. A well-
known actress who learned how to protect herself from the

control and manipulation of others spoke of the benefits of positive self-valuation. Early in her career she was told she had Multiple Sclerosis. At the same time, she realized that the insurance and entertainment industries would hire her when she limped only *if* she said she had been in an auto accident. Apparently, those entertainers who admit to having MS are not hired because of prejudices or insurance worries—namely that there will be many missed days of work or worse. This actress kept her disease, and her pain, to herself. As a result, she worked steadily. Of her choice she said, "I discovered that by keeping my illness a secret, I stayed in control of my life."

By thinking well of herself, by keeping her own counsel in this highly personal, sensitive matter, she took charge of her life—at least at the point of keeping the option to work. But only an individual with positive self-esteem and high integrity makes this sort of choice wisely. Another, someone who lacks this degree of self-worth and personal responsibility, may ultimately choose in a self-defeating manner. He abandons proper discretionary power and wisdom, as if he would shoot himself in the foot. As Abraham Maslow rightly taught, only to the actualized person (the one who has developed healthy degrees of self-knowledge and discipline) can we say, paraphrasing Maslow himself, "Choose what you will and it will probably be all right."

Even here there are no guarantees. When all is said and done, we have to take our chances. As we choose in ways we sense are right and good for us we must keep in mind that we alone are responsible for the consequences. Hopefully, we will have the discernment to choose in ways that empower us to contribute to ourselves *as well as to others.*

An unmarried couple conceived a child. The woman wanted to keep the baby, the father of the child did not. She agreed to an abortion, then—bitterly resentful of his influence on her—left the man, angry to this day. She blames him for the abortion and said she can never be happy. Morality aside, she had other options. Blaming another, we fail to take the responsibility for our choice, and deny our own power to choose. Were we to examine our motives, fears and feelings honestly we would realize that behind each choice—however hard it is—is a gift waiting: a gift of our own humanity, and affirmation. Life-affirming power.

In their most thorough book, *The Choicemaker*, authors Howes and Moon eloquently speak of the pull between the yes-no of a choice;

> . . . all of us spend untold amounts of energy resisting the serpent, resisting the risks, trying desperately to stay innocent and secure in the garden. We hold on to dependence, try to avoid decisions, grasp at comforting dreams and substitute drugs or doctrines for the hard task of choosing to know and to do. (Howes and Moon, 1973, p. 39)

By continually seeking guidance from without, by allowing ourselves to be unduly influenced by those important to us, we keep ourselves irresponsible and thus keep ourselves from becoming fully human. When we fail to take the necessary steps (or the consequences of those steps), when we fail to move our life along under our own command, we also deny ourselves power, commitment, a life of our own.

Yet be assured, especially in the early stages of our self-definitional choices, guidance may be appropriate. This is especially so if we are making major life-changes, facing a crisis or feeling intense emotions and interior upheaval when faced with options. Then emotional or spiritual direction, with a credible and trained person, is warranted. Therapy can help, provided—as mentioned—as an end-point goal, we learn how to become self-reliant, how to stand upon our own two feet and learn how to develop our discernment and decision-making powers.

All of us probably know that ultimately there are no assurances in life that what we choose to be or do is "right." Still, it is also human and completely natural to worry about what people will say if we do this or that or worry if we are going about things effectively. But too much worry is counter-productive. This saps energy and attention from worthwhile goals. In the end, what we do with our attention has a great deal to do with how we spend our life.

A friend and I discussed this very topic the other night. My friend admitted that he felt more useful to others than he was to himself. He said he just couldn't get his "act" together, that he was embarrassed because his family, especially his children, might think him a fool. He is neither an artistic nor a business success and feels self-conscious about this. I told him I didn't think I had my act together either, and moreover that I didn't really know what it was supposed to be. Aloud I wondered whether *our act* is life's important issue. Perhaps, instead of occupying ourselves with our act, we should notice whether or not we are giving something valuable to others, from within ourselves. Perhaps this is how our "act" becomes defined.

Do we help people? Are we encouraging to them? Do we contribute each day to the greater good in some small way? Can we forget ourselves, give up our self-consciousness, develop our best self so that others benefit? Can we curtail self-preoccupation, posturing and endless self-involvement long enough to function effectively during the day? If we grow in these areas, we can steadfastly develop power and ability. Then our act may clarify itself.

Perhaps, in the final analysis, no one really cares about

"our act." Our thinking about it may be just a trap. Perhaps the only helpful way to polish up our act is to discern how we might most easily, naturally and fulfillingly add value to the lives of others and then get on with doing that. Indeed this seems a guidepost to one more elegant choice.

4

Foolish Wisdom in the
Pursuit of Happiness

Life, willing to surpass itself, is the good life, and the good
life is the courageous life.

Paul Tillich, *The Courage To Be*

Einstein once wrote that those who search for happiness are
not worth much as persons. I think he meant that in the
pursuit of our own happiness we narrow our horizons, limit
ourselves to our petty ego concerns rather than opening ourselves up to others or to relevant world issues. Yet the quest
for happiness continues. Sometimes it seems to me we search
because we want to do justice to our life, want to "do it
right."

Happy people however don't think much about how they
got that way. Neither do they pay much attention to the pre-
cepts of others about paths to happiness. They are too busy
living fully. They *feel*, more than they can precisely articulate,
their life's intent, then faithfully follow this dimly lit subjective
light, doing whatever they can and must to express their life
meaningfully. In order to accomplish this, they must be willing to surpass themselves courageously. Happiness is rarely
their main concern. Yet usually it arrives as a by-product of
their vital life-expression.

THE VITAL LIFE EXPRESSION

What I call "vital life expression" is the way to happiness, although it is an indirect route and there are certainly no guarantees that good feelings will be our reward. Vital life expression means the self-affirmed, authentically lived life in which individually we discover our life's meaning and choose incrementally to live that knowledge out. For each of us vital life expression can be stalled, or even unimpressive. When we wonder what is a right course for us, when we feel stuck, when we sense we have made a wrong turn somewhere, followed the unhelpful impulse, when we compare ourselves to others who are more famous or prosperous than we are (always a mistake) then self-doubts naturally arise. With them our vitality is lessened. I know very few people, happy ones included, who don't spend some time wondering if they are honoring their lives properly.

The renowned essayist Logan Pearsall Smith wrote of his own self-doubts in a flawless little text titled *All Trivia:*

> 'And what are you doing now?' The question of these school contemporaries of mine, and their greeting the other day . . . (I remember how shabby I felt as I stood talking to them)—for a day or two that question haunted me. And behind their well-bred voices I seemed to hear the voice of Schoolmasters and Tutors, of the Professional Classes, and indeed of all the world. What, as a plain matter of fact, was I doing? How did I spend my days? (Smith, 1934, p. 60)

Smith tells us that instead of spending time in significant ways, so that people (what he calls "my contemporaries") should treat him as an important person, the day itself is enough for him:

But alas, the Day, the little Day, was enough just then. It somehow seemed enough, just to be alive in the Spring, with the young green of the trees, the smell of smoke in the sunshine; I loved the old shops and books, the uproar darkening and brightening in the shabby daylight. Just a run of good-looking faces—I was always looking for faces—would keep me amused. (Ibid.)

Persons, like Logan Pearsall Smith, who appreciate the moment, who have consciously chosen to trim their life's activities so that they have time to be thankful indwellers of the present, often seem foolish—even to themselves. These are the dreamers, putterers and gentle observers of the world who choose to ignore what Smith called "The Voice of The World." But in their foolishness I see a kind of higher wisdom, a touch of the divine: they are happy.

Another fine essayist, Robert Grundin, addresses this issue in another fashion in his lovely book, *Time & The Art of Living:*

The extent to which we live from day to day, from week to week, intent on details and oblivious to larger presences, is a gauge of our impoverishment in time. We drive through long stretches of magnificent country, less with pleasure than anxiety and fatigue, and come away bearing only the jumbled images of stop signs, passing lanes and gas stations. Deprived of the continuum, we lose not only the sole valid alternative to a present-centered existence, but also the nourishing context which can give substance and value to the present itself. (Grundin, 1982, p. 6)

A predictable irony to the 'how to be happy' question is that to live our answers, individually, may require that we contradict majority opinion on the subject. This trust operates in every conceivable direction. In fact, there seems no way to please people, so a first rule of thumb is not to try. People who consciously take time to live quietly and simply, who prefer, for example, to play instead of work, are generally criticized for their lack of industry.

Then again, those who fall hopelessly in love with their art, craft, families, or livelihoods, who consider what they do high calling, in the old-fashioned devotional sense, are also scolded by The Voice of The World for being "too serious." They get in trouble for not playing enough. They are rudely, and often erroneously labeled "workaholics," platitudinously advised to "take time out to smell the roses." This saying, now banal, has as much import as the merchant's refrain, "Have a nice day."

A personal case in point (I find myself cautioned and advised at every turn, usually by those I hardly know): a dear friend introduced me to a charming elderly woman. For some reason, probably because she herself enjoyed a few days there, she wanted me to visit an island in the Pacific Northwest when she heard I planned a trip north. During an otherwise cozy and delicious dinner, she brought out maps, postcards and photographs of the place. I had my own plans for my trip—which I never had a chance to discuss—and when I tried to say, ever so gently, that I might not have time to visit the island, she sternly instructed: "Two days isn't enough time to see the place. You budget your time so you have time enough for travel." Her tone reminded me of the words of another friend who once told me her family called her "selfish" whenever her plans went against theirs.

Not only do we go against the grain of world-opinion when we choose self-affirmingly, but also we may consciously choose things that temporarily create discomfort and inconvenience for ourselves. To be happy in the long run we find we choose discomfort in the short run. The dieter who forgoes sweets for a time in order to shed weight, the person who tells her spouse the truth about her waning love for him, the individual who, despite fear, visits the dentist, are all examples of persons choosing to do the distasteful thing in order to live the good life.

Self-affirmation, as I have described it, requires us to act upon what we know to be our values, virtues, and honest aspirations. To do this we must strengthen the muscles of our very existence. This requires risk-taking skill.

Nietzsche wrote that if we will to have life it meant we must also will to have power. He meant *personal power*, the sort that enables us to be in our own corner when others aren't, the power that lets us choose to do the terrifying, necessary or morally right thing. Power like this is gained at a cost. When we are cowardly, we dare not take risks—even small and intellectually, safe, appropriate ones. When we are cowardly, we fear everything. Yet if we want to live fully, beyond the life we have today, we must take risks, stretch ourselves, move past what we are now. From these choices, power is gradually gained.

I know a man who was painfully shy. To do work in a way he valued he had to consciously choose to push beyond his conception of himself as a shy, inward sort. This choice—the choice to push or not to push ourselves in a matter—is a most personal one. If we don't push enough we stagnate and rot. If we push too hard we brutalize ourselves at the very time we need our own love and self-support. Only the individual himself knows when to start or stop pushing, when to forge ahead or stop entirely.

My shy friend is now able to enter completely unfamiliar environments, make friends easily (and in a way that helps others feel at ease) and is quite outgoing because he chose courageously. He willed to have his life expand, chose to have his life surpass itself.

If we seek too much comfort, if we avoid pain, risks, possible humiliation, embarrassment, awkwardness, we cannot—it seems to me—expect happiness. Our self-protective choices will necessarily deliver the reverse because the natural order of things seems to require a sacrifice of safety, the familiar, security.

BLISS, BEING AND HAPPINESS

Despite Einstein's discounting the pursuit of happiness, I find myself dwelling on this subject. In part, this is because countless readers write asking "how" they can find happiness. One man, representing others, wrote in response to my previous book on right livelihood:

> I believe it was Joseph Campbell who said, 'Follow your bliss,' do what makes you happy, no matter what it is and the money will follow. Don't worry about money, it will follow.
>
> I don't doubt these words, nor do I doubt yours. My question is: how do you know what makes you happy? How do you find out where your bliss is?
>
> What, if any, are the mechanisms that you know of whereby a person can honestly tap into that inner resource of himself to discover where his bliss and right work lie? This seems to be a very difficult process.

My initial answer is this: we *can* know what makes us happy. At the very least, we can know what we prefer to be, to do or to have. We can tap into a part of ourselves—an inner reservoir of knowledge, quite subterranean, quite hidden— that holds all our answers. The greater our awareness (and here I mean general awareness, our awakeness if you wish) the greater likelihood that we will experience bliss of the sort this reader wants to find. The two, awareness and bliss, are natural partners. The more we simply *are*, for instance, the more bliss we experience.

The other night I was visiting some friends. At a point in the evening we were sitting around, gazing into the fireplace, which was burning warmly and prettily, discussing rather mundane matters such as vacations, birding and mutual ac- quaintances. Quite suddenly I experienced my companions with new appreciation, felt new and deeper levels of affection for them, came into the present moment in an unabashedly lov- ing way. I felt happy, beyond my ability to describe it now, and this quality could rightly be termed "bliss." Looking back I believe the moment grew immensely significant; each person there became immensely meaningful to me because, for what- ever lucky reason, I grew immensely aware, came into the mo- ment with greater consciousness than before.

People who meditate or pray know about this, although in different fashion perhaps, as do those who practice some sort of solitary discipline, such as long-distance running. The one who prays profoundly, the yoga enthusiast, the mindful nature walker all slip into a blissful state, however momentary, when their self-absorption ceases and they move beyond into an ec- statically present state—and be assured that this is what it is.

This moment gives us clues about "how" to be happy. Be- yond self-consciousness, in the realms of self-forgetfulness and high involvement with projects that hold fascination for us, we transcend our small egoistic self. There we may find happi- ness, and if not that, then, even better, joy.

Only that empty state of mind, where we ourselves are absent, paradoxically most fully present, brings happiness. But if we search for it, happiness usually eludes us. Absorption is the key, but absorption with something outside ourselves: a craft, service, creation—these functions allow us to become en- thralled and lovingly involved with what we do, take us out of our mind's preoccupation with our own interests, lead us to a fruitful state of being.

This is perhaps one reason why those who are "on fire" to accomplish something important to them (whatever it might be, from baking a cake or building a cabinet to finding a cure for some disease) are also persons who, when asked, admit to being happy. Whether it is joy, high level optimism or positive energy that they possess, however they describe these pleasant feelings, these carry them over the hard times, help them survive, move them through the ordeal and the ordinary.

Surely it is this state, even if only in part, that lets us focus on others (instead of on ourselves) and brings us into that present-centered existence wherein bliss resides.

When I was a child I had to live with a relative who was, for all intents and purposes, psychically "absent." In our midst physically, she was, as the saying goes, not at home psychologically. Her blank, vacant stare told the story, and a scary one it was.

I still sinkingly remember how awful it was to try to talk with her. Again and again I tried, only to hear her mumble strangely to someone other than me (there was no one else around). Her self-involvement was so complete that she needed no one else to talk to. Her construct of reality comprised herself alone (and some shadowy, bodyless entities she scolded, feared and related to). But these entities were shadowy figments of her weird, no doubt chemically imbalanced imagination. Not surprisingly, this was not a "happy" person. She did not live the good life.

ON THE IRRELEVANCE OF HAPPINESS

Paul Tillich writes that the good life is the courageous life, the life we have when we let ourselves surpass ourselves. It is, he tells us, the life of the "powerful soul," the "triumphant body," whose enjoyment comes from virtue. (Tillich, 1952) I agree, and think this not too different from what I have been saying in these pages. Perhaps a certain measure of arrogance and audacity are needed if we are to live such a life. For one thing, we must necessarily ask ourselves some tough questions:

♦ What values, what virtues, what qualities do I want to embody in and through my choices and myself?

♦ What do I want to do with my life when all is said and done?

♦ When do I feel best about myself?

♦ What is fulfilling for me to do?

♦ When have I been so fully engrossed in an activity that time and space were lost on me?

♦ In what ways can my life, the life in me, surpass itself?

If we answer honestly and without censorship or pretended modesty we may see that certain activities and people raise our awareness and aliveness while others put us to sleep, create defensive responses, or take harmony and inner balance from our lives. If, like our reader, we wonder "how" to be happy, we may want to examine the way in which our own choices add to or deplete our personal power.

To attain long-lasting happiness, not just fleeting slivers of bliss, our most deeply planted life-intentions must find expression through us. Again, some people—the happiest— seem to "know" what directions to take to self-affirm themselves in this way.

One such person is a man who decided to start a private consulting practice while he was still relatively young. He says:

I started management consulting at age 22 for a large hospital in Boston. Today, I'm on my own, as a health care expert, struggling but happy. Very happy. I'm still in health care, but from a different angle: as an advisor to hospitals and healing centers. My own personal belief is that no one knows better than himself what is best for his development . . .

I feel that the best I can do as a business consultant is to bring people closer to that part of them that 'knows' what to do and then support them as they learn this for themselves, while at the same time providing them with the systems and procedures to do just that.

When I interviewed him about "how" he knows what makes him happy, he said he didn't know *how*. He said his knowing was related to how he felt and how engaged he was in what he was doing. He also knows when he is not happy. When I asked if he had an image or inner vision toward which he moved—even if a vague one—he admitted that when he was a child he had drawn pictures of a health care facility of some kind. Later on, he had written down ideas about his image, and these had guided his goal-seeking activities as a young man.

I've never deviated from the overall sense of what I had to do, including when I left the consulting job in the Boston hospital. I knew all along that I needed to do some internal body work and that this would unfold naturally for me. But I can't tell you *how* I knew.

In listening to him and observing my own life path, I feel we are all much like the characters in Steven Spielberg's film "Close Encounters of a Third Kind." The hero, heroine and several others share a compelling inner sense that they *must* get to a specific location immediately. On some level, they feel "invited" to this destination. Each holds an inner image of this place, which they then try to draw or sculpt. Others around them think they are crazy. But, regardless of the consequence, each one eventually risks his or her life to get to this place, their destiny—a desolate mountain top.

In the case of the man I interviewed, his "destiny" now involves working in a state-of-the-art healing center in Hawaii. He says, "It isn't as if I 'want' to do this—there is no will involved. I simply went inside myself and discovered something there that I felt I must share and express."

Through this kind of "knowing," by choosing to move toward the invitation to life we feel we have received, we help our highest self, or Self, ascend. In that process, we find happiness.

THE ABILITY TO ACT

Intentions count as nothing if we do not translate them into action. I know a man who is a brilliant thinker. He could be an excellent writer. He loves to write and has always said he wished he had the time to write. Now that he's retired, he has the time. But still he writes nothing. He complains that he has nothing to say. That is his dilemma.

If we are unhappy, perhaps we are in a similar fix. If we are to be happy, we must first decide what we want to do with our lives, intend to make it happen, and then we must begin to work on our intention.

As we proceed in our lives, acting more and more on our intentions to live out our purpose, we can notice some clear signals that indicate we are on the right developmental path. Our choices have a distinctive pattern to them:

♦ Our choices increasingly *enhance* our self-evaluation and self-esteem.

♦ Our choices *reinforce* our sense of worth and self-respect and improve the actual condition of everything around us.

♦ We become more self-sufficient, more able to think independently.

♦ We find ourselves progressively absorbed with the ideas, things, people, activities around us—experiencing these with delight.

♦ We increasingly act toward others with responsible, mature, stewardly love.

However, to get to the point of acting, we must first move out of our own apathy, inertia, dullness and deadness. It's there that the writer-to-be, mentioned above, remains stuck. It may be there that many who write to me remain. Before people can get unstuck they must ask themselves what they wish to say with their *life*. Only then will their choices begin to have a clear life message, with a strong unique character. Only in this way will self-forgetting be attainable, and—through it—happiness as a by-product.

OBSTACLES, EXCUSES, DIVERSIONS

The real difficulty may be that we can know what makes us happy, not that we can't. Unfortunately, many of us prefer *not* to know, because then we don't have to feel compelled to *act on* what is known. Not knowing keeps us safe, bland, invisible. The rigorous work is to attend to our inward cues and signals, sensitizing ourselves to what we already know. These inner cues can humble us: an ordinary life, one without glamor or spectacular success, may be our true desire. Or we may be destined to forego family or other ordinary longed-for satisfactions in order to contribute to the greater good. For this reason, we delay and avoid knowing what we want, what we are about as persons.

We set up enormous blocks to knowing our life's purpose, confusing and distracting ourselves with all sorts of worldly worries and preoccupations. We resist. An opportunity may come along, something we have been waiting for—say a promotion or a chance for relationship or adventurous travel—but we create reasons to avoid commitment.

One woman I interviewed is starting a national magazine. She was amazed when some of the people she had planned to hire on this new endeavor began to fall away.

> This is the chance of a lifetime for them—but they are so fearful. It's as if they want advice from me about what they should do. I try to 'worst case' it for them, to help them see that there really isn't such a risk involved. The worst thing that could happen is that they would have to find another job if this doesn't work out. But this terrifies them. My feeling is that their fear is deeper than the actual concern warranted.

She is right. Our fears are deeply embedded in our basic fear of life itself. The more we fear life—and by this I mean our own vitality and life-energies—the more we fear various specific things, whether it be death itself, ambiguous situations—flying, illness—or that we will be a victim of some horrible crime. Our fears and nameless worries are often unconscious screens that filter out the knowledge of what will make us happy. As we concentrate on our fears, anxieties, worries and neuroticisms, we distract ourselves from having to face facts we don't want to know; our distractions allow us time to avoid taking action on choices that make us happy.

The woman who started her own magazine had her fears too, but these didn't get in the way of what she knew she wanted to do. Once she made the decision to start her own publication, she realized that she *had* to go ahead.

> Actually, I had a huge fear of *not* doing this, rather than fearing what would happen if I did this and failed. I knew that if I didn't do this, there would be a dying inside me. For the rest of my life, something inside would be killing me.

Martin Buber once wrote that the word for Satan in Hebrew means "hinderer." The hinderer in each of us would have us believe that our happiness is hard, maybe impossible, to find. This is what creates the sense that we cannot find a life's purpose which is right and meaningful for us. This is the power of death—what psychologists call the death wish—residing in each of us. This wish or inclination works in many ways: it subjects us to an inclination to crawl contractedly through our days, turning our backs on our own delights, enthusiasms and highest ideals. Of course, some things in us *must* die for us to live robustly: our egocentric self-involvement, frailties, complainings, our irresponsibility and the pseudo-stupidity that says, "I don't know what makes me happy." It has been my observation that as people choose and live more boldly, their various fears diminish. The more they choose to live, the less fear they experience.

I repeat: not-knowing is a way to stay safe. Sometimes, for instance, we fear knowing ourselves as creative or gifted, because we are concerned about pleasing significant others in our lives, or fitting into "the system." Pushing ourselves to "know" can court disaster. Oftentimes society, friends, family, institutions, even organized religions do not take kindly to self-realized people. Someone's intensely lived life-purpose can become an irritation or affront to others. One woman told me that as she became more involved with activities that made her happier, her spouse became increasingly disconcerted.

> He's fine and loving when I need comforting. But when I'm excited about my own projects, he's not that thrilled. Maybe I'm too intense at those times. But he seems threatened by my strength of purpose, as if that will pull me away from depending on him. Well, it will. But lately I see, and I wish he could, that the more of myself I find, the more quality time and attention I have to give to him.

Also, as we grow stronger inwardly, we may become more opinionated. The petty involvements or gossip of our associates will no longer interest us. We develop a stronger sense of what we prefer. We make choices quickly. These choices integrate us at a higher level of functioning and allow us to use ourselves more fully than before. We spend time fruitfully. Perhaps we become quick to say what we really think.

A young actor-turned-director said that he had been asked to direct because he was strong-minded and opinionated. He admitted that this trait helped him at work, but didn't suit his friends.

> I've always known how I wanted things to be. So when our director took ill, I was asked by the producers if I could direct. I had no doubts, and I guess that's what sold them. I'd have to say I never had any doubts. This is a positive trait for me, but my friends—especially the ones who are unsure of themselves—are upset by my certainty.

Such confidence, even arrogance, can be hard on others. But we're not talking here about how to "win friends and influence people." We are examining how knowing and living out our life's purpose can *lead* to fulfillment. However, I want to be precisely understood in saying that by getting in touch with what we need in life and by developing a degree of confidence, we do *not* automatically become brazenly disruptive to others. Along with the "arrogance" of knowing what he or she wants, the self-realizing person simultaneously develops growing compassion, a tenderness and love for the other, feels the other "as-self." Still, I also must add that given the reality of social relationships, the creative, spirited person probably always feels at odds with society. One woman said, "In a way I am lonelier now—I don't really fit into a group anymore." Another, a priest, said he was often misunderstood by his colleagues. We should not be surprised if our joy is not synchronous with another's expectations of us. Nor should we be dismayed if, as we grow toward self-realization, we feel like a minority of one. But fortunately, these times of feeling like a misfit usually only happen during the superficial moments. In the significant arenas of life, we are now more intimately connected to others, never really alone.

Because of the *disadvantages* of knowing what we need to do with our life, we can feel ambivalent about discovering our life's purpose. Even introspection is clouded with confusion. As Maslow wrote, we are "simultaneously worms and gods." With penetrating insight, he described how society punishes women who try to search out and affirm their own good:

> Many brilliant women are caught up in the problem of making an unconscious identification between intelligence and masculinity. To probe, search, be curious . . . all these she may feel as defeminizing, especially if her husband in his uncertain masculinity is threatened. Many cultures and many religions have kept women from knowing and studying . . . to keep them 'feminine' (in a sadomasochistic sense); for instance, women cannot be priests and rabbis. (Maslow, 1962, p. 59)

Maslow also reminded us that many humans—from the timid youngster to the well-mannered adult—learn that "success" is synonymous with *not* asking, with accommodating adjustment, with sociable behavior. Growing into one's own person means challenging others—and therefore is dangerous. People who are "too confident" are likely to make trouble— they ask questions of those in authority, they say what they prefer even when not asked, they don't allow themselves to be exploited.*

Perhaps *we* can see how choosing, *intending*, to express our life purpose can create discomfort—in us and in others. Indeed, we may need to *train* ourselves to feel comfortable about being energized around our own purposes. It may take some self-coaching to feel that it is all right to leave thankless jobs or relationships or abusive situations that we thought to be our lot in life. To be sure, liberating ourselves for true fulfillment *will* cost us something—comfort, money, time, the approval of family members or old friends. But if our ultimate goal is to know ourselves and to live out that knowledge so as to benefit ourselves and others, then we can not have, as an automatic first goal, to live in ways that please others.

INNER DIVISIONS

Not all obstacles to self-knowledge stem from worrying about offending or disrupting others. Some blocks arise from our own inner divisions. We may, for example, feel guilty about being happy—feel that we don't deserve to be happy. Thus we recoil from it. I am reminded of a folk-tale I heard as

---

*I have written at length about the ramifications of increasing numbers of actualizing adults in the workplace and about why such adults are hard to "manage." (Sinetar, 1987)

a student about peasant mothers of perfectly healthy, beautiful children. It seems that women, in centuries past, would carry their beautiful infants up to a mountain top to cry out to the gods that their children were defective. In this way they hoped to stave off the jealousy of the gods, which might be stirred if a human child were "too good," too capable of competing with the gods. Prometheus, who attempted to steal fire from the gods and who was punished for this, serves as another mythological reminder of the dangers of trying to steal power or knowledge from the gods.

Even the legendary Adam and Eve portray a sinful nature because they attempted to gain knowledge by eating of the fruit of the tree of knowledge. They teach an important lesson to those of us who study such things. We could interpret (and many have) their fall from grace as having happened because they tried to know what God knew—that they, like Prometheus, tried to be like God.

But another interpretation is to see their sin as their descent into a lesser consciousness—into *unbelief*. Their grave error may have been in trying to possess something they already had. God, we are told, had given them everything: the whole world was theirs. Their essential flaw was in *choosing* to disobey God's instruction and in doubting the fullness of the good they already had. They gave in to Satan's manipulations when they doubted, when they felt they needed more. In fact, within the garden, within themselves—they already *had* all. This lie— that there was something more they needed—replaced their original fullness of heart and mind. Thus they *chose unreality* (lack, doubt, deficit, etc.) over reality. Many human beings continue to choose in this way.

Even for us, as contemporary adults, knowing ourselves and identifying what brings us fulfillment and happiness may seem akin to stealing from God. This is especially so if we have learned that we must please others or if we have been taught that knowing ourselves is dangerous or difficult. In this case we will be guilt-ridden when trying to live our life so that we honor what we truly value. We then choose so as not to offend others. Or we search endlessly for "happiness," thinking that someone else has answers we need. But, in actuality, any knowledge we need we already have: within us. Could it be that our error is in striving for something we already have? Perhaps, like Adam and Eve, we too must let go of our self-imposed unreality and live out the good we already possess by *choosing* only in the direction of what we *know* to be our good.

Sometimes, for example, we try too hard to figure things out logically. We strive to find concrete reassurances, try to bolster our fragmented self with things that will make us feel safe from the outside: the advice of experts, money in the bank, relationships with strong, dominant people who can protect and take care of us. We buy into a lie (i.e., that we don't have within ourselves the power and knowledge to stand on our own two feet), and live our lives impotently and uncreatively. For our unbelief, we pay a steep price: unhappiness. Its forms are endless.

Our fragmented self is our biggest hindrance, and blocks our ability to act smoothly, in spontaneous synchrony with what we intuitively know is right, true and good for us. Then we end up mired in inertia and lifelessness. We live as if dead.

While fragmented we *feel* deficient because we *are* deficient. We make wrong choices, because we have failed to grow into our own innate intuitive ability to *know* ourselves as whole. This knowledge brings fulfillment. While fragmented we need experts, strong people, status symbols and logical arguments to bolster us, to fill up what Maslow called "empty holes." These holes must be filled before we can have peace. And, of course, neediness such as this mushrooms: insatiably, we crave assurance, outer supports and directives the more we believe in our deficits. We forfeit our capacity to live dynamically with full, spontaneous use of our instincts and intuitions by failing to choose as if we were whole. "Let the weak say 'I am strong,' " Scripture teaches. But when we are deficit we don't believe this.

While fragmented, we also cultivate the belief that happiness is elusive, found only outside ourselves—in hard-to-locate solutions, in material things or in other people. The truth is, externals never make us safer, stronger or better as persons. In reality, it is the other way around, as Saint Augustine pointed out in his treatise, *On Free Choice of the Will*:

> The man who makes evil use (of things) clings to them with love and is entangled by them, (that is, he becomes subject to those things which ought to be subject to him, and creates for himself good whose right and proper use requires that he himself be good.) They do not make him good or better, but become better because of him. (St. Augustine, 1964 ed., p. 33)

Every*thing* in the world—material possessions, the communities we live in, the jobs we hold—is created *for* us. Everything and everyone should grow better *because* of us. We must not look to things or people to make us feel more alive. Nor should we look to outer sources to show us how to be happy, or to *be* our happiness. That only produces dis-ease, lovelessness and powerlessness because it is based on a lie of deficit.

Take, for example, the case of a woman who is abused by her spouse or lover. If he convinces her—that is, if she *accepts* his logic—that she cannot help herself, she is lost. She invites invasion again and again, along with diminished self-esteem and greater fear—all the while growing in the belief that she *needs him*, must stay with him. She is the author of her own demise.

This is an extreme example of how our personal fragmentation, our own split, destroys us and drains us of our livingness. We may not carry matters as far as the abused woman, yet we too allow our life energies to dissipate in lesser ways. We waste time in social situations that mean nothing to us because we think we *need* the social connections. We placate family members who terrorize us because we feel we *need* their love and attention, or because we fear the comments of others were we to go our own way. We chase after "happiness," on a quest for more glamorous careers, places and times. And as we do so, happiness becomes ever more elusive.

But when we are in our right minds, we know that happiness comes from our own wholeness, from our right choices and from the correct, disciplined use of our talents. As I see it, following that knowing—or foolish wisdom, if you prefer—is not arrogance. Rather our true arrogance is in our repeated and willful denial of what we already know and our rejection of what we have been given. Being—expressing ourselves as whole and complete—is our indicated action for gaining happiness.

That's not to say—and I want to be clear about this—that following our foolish wisdom means dashing off in some new direction on some impulse to "do our thing." I am speaking about a much deeper level, a transcendent level, of knowing and acting. This demands the purest thought and introspection, as well as time and patience. In waiting, in patient reflection, we ready ourselves as if for a grace. Thomas Merton advises us along these lines:

> With respect to the higher freedom of grace, our natural freedom is simply a potency waiting to be developed. . . . Grace does not take hold of us as if we were planes or rockets guided by remote control. (Merton, 1961, pp. 44–45)

Besides being patient with ourselves and giving ourselves the time we need to live and grow in this way, we must remember that it is no shame to be afraid. As we listen more intently to our life-spirit, we find ourselves having to choose between the known and unknown. We may need to let go of friends, habits, work, a residence or ways of being in order to travel toward our stronger, more complete self. Such changes can be terrifying, at least at first. It is perfectly natural in these circumstances to cling to safety. We must respect this natural instinct for security. To be too harsh with ourselves is to court regression.

Learning to listen to the spirit of life in us does not mean we abruptly turn our lives upside down, today. Listening inward does not mean making instant or revolutionary choices, or proceeding full steam ahead without respecting the dangers of growth.

In very small ways, at every point in our day, we can choose conservatively, yet steadily, to express a new-found maturity or wholeness. In small inconsequential ways we deny those needs which have crippled us in the past. Every human has both sets of impulses within: the impulse for growth and the one for safety or stability. If we push too much, as I have tried to say elsewhere, we run the risk of impairing our future growth. It is not so much *what* we do—in terms of practical actions—that move us toward wholeness but how we think about ourselves that counts. Do we, for example, think of ourselves as strong, able, creative, competent? Or do we hold a deficit image of ourselves. More than pace of growth, belief in the fullness of what we have in us, already, moves us forward, attracts to us our good.

5

Beyond Fear

> . . . the way to build self-confidence is to start doing things you're not sure you can do. Like flirting with strangers. Like baking your own bread. Like painting a picture. . . . Do it. Seize the day and get started and stay with it, and things will get easier and easier from here.
>
> Paul Williams, *Das Energi*

Each of us makes life's difficult choices differently. As we move closer to being our whole and distinctive self, patterns emerge in productive, life-enhancing choices which seem to have a predictable sequence:

♦ We choose in a wholesome direction *despite* feelings of fear or our need to cling to the familiar. We somehow push ahead, even if minutely, in a line we sense to be intrinsically "right" or "true." Over time, fear ceases to be our prime motivator.

♦ In a closely related way, reactive choice-making diminishes and finally—if we are well-developed, mature persons— may end entirely. Instead of avoiding those things we fear, we start pro-actively selecting those ways of being, thinking and acting that most efficiently take us toward what we consciously want. Our choices are less convoluted, become a straighter line of action to the goals we want to achieve within our deepest, intentional self.

♦ Our self-acceptance for our truest, "living self" increases. We find, gradually for the most part, that whatever we sense ourselves to be at the core—both desirable and undesirable—we can outwardly be "the self I am." However flawed, we move to present our real self to others, to live our real selves in our lives.

♦ Ultimately, our choices *flow* from this core-self, instead of being *forced*. Each choice somehow effortlessly stems from our more coherent, consistent self-and-world view. Our small choices lead, incrementally, to larger more vivid and self-defining ones. However painful, our tough life-choices further our interior person and highest standard of conduct. We are faithfully courageous and loving toward ourselves and—eventually—toward others.

Growing more closely attuned to our inner workings, we also grow more conscious and self-accepting. In bursts, we develop keen insight and then appreciation for the sly ways in which we hold ourselves back. Soon we notice how our negative feelings can actually *help* us, provide information to us much as a mirror or photograph. We release various pent-up energies within as some bit of paralysis dissolves.

"Best choices," however much they involve loss or letting go, allow us to feel more potent, creative and optimistic about ourselves. All insight is energizing. One woman, who became aware of an emerging pattern to her best choices, helps us compare our own growth with her healthful lines:

> My life-supportive choices are characterized by a definite pattern. This pattern is usually difficult and painful because it involves letting go of "shoulds" and also saying goodbye to people I cared about who remained comfortable with those "shoulds." But once I have worked through

the transition period, I do not regret making these choices, even though it has never been easy.

These choices always center around issues of personal integrity, personal identity, creative self-expression and a universal consciousness. Also, recognizing a life-supportive choice has often been intuitive and instantly "knowable" for me.

As her comments reveal, we can subjectively know—spontaneously and almost instantly—what we want to do in a matter, or what we must do. However, taking the steps toward that knowledge is often slow-going. We harm ourselves badly by expecting ourselves to follow any preset schedule of action. In my own life, I have yearned to do things that I *knew* I would only be able to do decades later. I have continually had to face my limitations squarely and accept my own inability to act, my insecurities or dependencies, even though I have not liked looking at what I saw.

Waiting for such time as I am ready to act on what I sense is the right course has enabled me, actually forced me, to develop a degree of patience I never knew I had. While my idealized version of myself imagines that I can instantly act out my ideas, desires or goals, my real self—that person who really lives inside my skin—is often too timid or frightened to move ahead swiftly. Learning to accept that inner person has taught me something about love.

Everyone has his or her own rate of speed when it comes to making difficult life-choices. One person said this:

The choices I have forced in my life have not been as successful or as right for me as the ones that came as a result of sudden insight. It seems as if I just gave in to the circumstance, let go, and "Wham!"—the decision was made.

The less effort I gave the decision, the easier it was, and the better it was in the long run.

Another person's tempo is completely different. Her best choices come only after much intense labor and thinking.

Usually these involved an almost complete reversal of life-direction: marrying after having planned never to; becoming a teacher when it was the one thing I was sure I would never do; withdrawing from our local church when parish life was a number one priority for our family . . . and now, separating from my husband after twenty-six years of marriage.

Thus, while our life-supportive choices can follow the sequence described at the beginning of this chapter, we should keep in mind that each of us moves through this sequence at an individualized pace. This is a crucial point to remember while reading the rest of this chapter, as we explore the various stages of the developmental progression of life-supportive choice-making.

MOVING BEYOND FEAR

Fear makes us feel helpless. We experience ourselves as out of control or "on the brink." These feelings remind us of terrifying times when we were small and truly dependent on others (perhaps others who were not as responsible with us as we are currently with ourselves). Our fear returns us to memories of times when we really were powerless. During these times an advisor or trusted friend can be an objective, detached sounding board. They assist us by simply *being* with us. Self-acceptance, a topic we return to repeatedly in connection with the whole issue of managing fear, is also a valuable attitude to possess and cultivate in ourselves. For example, we may find that we hold too much inner resistance to move ahead with our original plans. In this case, rather than berating ourselves, we may find it preferable to step back and observe ourselves (through journal-keeping, counseling sessions, a support group of some sort) for a while until our feelings of helplessness and anxiousness subside.

Such was the case with a woman who had been trying for years to start a small home-business. Something about that venture frightened her. A former executive secretary, she had given up her career when she had married. She stayed home to raise a large family. As the children grew, she knew she wanted to use her business skills to the fullest, but worried constantly about what she could *not* do, about what might go wrong, about how she might not be adequate to the task of building a reputable business. Years passed and she did nothing to further her original ambitions. She finally admitted she was stuck and began to move along completely different lines. She started working in a journal, daily logging in her thoughts and ideas about life. She jotted down her impressions about her reading, which was also important to her at this time. Within a few months, her journal became increasingly vital in her life—her primary growth tool. Through it she grew more comfortable with herself and learned to trust her intuitions, her subjective life and her innate good sense. One day she surprised herself by writing out a business plan for a service-venture she could conduct out of her kitchen. She said of this experience:

> I'd fretted for so many years, worrying about what I couldn't do, that I'd overlooked what I could do. Instead of letting my fears dominate me, as was my norm, I realized I was listing action steps to take me where I wanted

to go. This new ambition is a far-off place, much larger and expanded than the one I used to have, and I feel certain that I can reach it. I'm more energized than I can tell you and all sorts of little aches and pains that I have had also eased up.

The irony of it all is that I hadn't noticed myself changing. But as my confidence grew, I allowed myself to think of what I wanted. Instead of trying to eliminate all risks, I moved prudently toward what I wanted. Previously I thought only of avoiding error. So I was paralyzed. My fear images were too vivid; I let myself use these to stay in place. Now I go directly toward my goals. It's so much more efficient!

As this woman's story illustrates, fear can be a major barrier to choosing rightly. We may *know* what we need to do, but we also know we are quite terrified to act on behalf of what we know. This fear is illogical yet all-consuming. We hesitate, procrastinate, rationalize and dissuade ourselves from going ahead with even our simplest plans. We try everything except patient self-acceptance and love!

Ironically, if we could just accept ourselves as fearful, if we could simply embrace ourselves *as we are*, if we could tell ourselves the truth about what is happening within our subjective selves—as a way of self-support and stabilization—we could cancel much of our fear, even if we do nothing actively to move against it. Somehow, beneath the surface of our conscious selves, we take notice that someone has loved us enough to be accepting. This someone is our *self*. Because at the very least we know ourselves as truthful, solid and in our own corner, fear subsides. Because the scriptural adage, "Love never fails," is absolutely accurate, the stance of self-acceptance and self-support always provides a measure of interior repair and healing, even if an invisible measure.

Moving beyond fear only happens if and as we give ourselves permission to *feel* our fears and anxieties. The absolute first-step in resolving these uncomfortable feelings is to admit we have them, to know that fearfulness is a natural human response and that it serves a healthy purpose: to protect us from danger, threats and life-defeating circumstances. Our struggles with self-doubt or fear or other nameless worries are often made much worse by denying we have such feelings. Even worse, we may be so cut off from our feeling-life, our subjective self, that we don't even know *what* we feel.

If, on the other hand, we can summon up the courage to face ourselves as living, human beings, we quickly realize that traumatic life-choices (which may require loss, separation from loved ones or familiar ways of doing things) carry with them grave and very real practical considerations. These are significant issues to anyone, and our feelings provide us with valuable information about how to proceed.

Some people push themselves too stridently to be courageous. When I have done this it is usually because I have an image in my mind about how I'm "supposed" to behave. I try too bravely to conform to this rigid ideal. I now find myself opposed to therapies that involve force, just as I am opposed to forcing small children, who fear water, into the deep, dark end of the pool. This tactic seems unnecessarily harsh and brutal. If we simply look our fear in the face, simply accepting without judgment that we are upset about something, and taking time to make that choice (provided that we have the time, of course), usually the choice is made without so much pain.

If we ignore unpleasant feelings, or deny the fact that we are waking up at three in the morning, unable to sleep because of worry, or if we tell ourselves that as adults we need not behave so childishly, we easily damage ourselves. *To move beyond fear we must pay attention to it, accept that it serves a useful purpose in our lives, and accept ourselves at the very* **point** *of our fear*. By this

I mean we have to know *what* we feel and *where* in us our fear resides, and grasp *what* its peculiar tone may be. These understandings are then the specific areas which demand our nurturing attitudes in order for growth to occur.

A man whom I had never met phoned me, greatly troubled by his decision to quit a secure salesman position. He wanted to open a bookstore, but didn't have enough money. He was prepared to take a cut in salary. Having recently turned forty-five, he felt time was "running out" on his life. He was pushing himself to move quickly. He apparently had been inspired by the many success stories he'd read about small business owners and felt this was the way to go. Still he was in a panic. I could hear it in his voice, and he admitted this was so. Fortunately for him, he had the good sense to phone. He was blessed that he didn't discount his feelings. He told me he was afraid of using up his life-savings. I, in turn, told him that this was a very practical consideration and cautioned him to take more time before quitting his job. I asked him if he'd given thought to retaining a part-time position in order to stabilize himself financially, since a part-time job seems an excellent way of maintaining some sense of security while transitioning into a new way of life. He had not considered this. Further discussion proved that his decision-making process might have been contaminated by his eagerness to get going; he, in fact, really preferred to work part-time. Since he was a top salesman in a high-tech field, he was in an ideal position to negotiate the shorter job-hours with his present employer. Again, his voice betrayed his feelings: he sounded relieved and optimistic at the end of our conversation.

The point I underscore is that his fear was a sound warning device for him. He had attended to it, if only by phoning. Moreover, by his openness and candor, I sensed he left our conversation with the beginnings of a more strategic, sensible approach to his career choices. I never heard from him again.

Perhaps all he needed, as each of us does from time to time, was a bit of encouragement and permission to take his fears seriously. He heard me say he must not brow-beat himself into a mistaken notion of what achievement "should" be.

A first rule for managing fear is this: *do not ignore it.* Fear reminds us that something important to our lives or to our survival is at stake. The next rule is to raise our awareness about our fear (or whatever negative emotions dominate our decision-making). Perhaps our fear is unwarranted. Perhaps we only need to talk to an objective other who can be a sounding board, helping us put things in perspective. Just because we feel frightened does not mean we have to stop moving ahead. Fear means we should pay attention.

The *intensity* of our fear is another factor to which we should attend. Intense fear indicates something is amiss. The degree to which we are experiencing either physical or emotional upset helps us better gauge whether to seek counsel, talk to a trusted friend, or whether to abandon ship. The healthier we are, the likelier it is we will move gently *with* our feelings, as if we were in a dance of sorts. Healthy persons allow themselves some rest when they need it. They reach out to those whom they trust. They ask for, and are receptive to, guidance and reassurance. They remember how, when they were small, they overcame fearful, helpless states and moved beyond them. They use friends, information, supportive "self-talk" to nurture and reassure themselves.

Dr. David Viscott, whose book *The Language of Feelings* I often recommend, provides sound practical advice about dealing with fear:

> Fear, like all feelings, serves an important purpose—in this case, to alert us to defend ourselves. So when people try to pretend they're not afraid, they seldom do themselves any good. Fear protects us, and we ignore it at our peril,

whether out of a desire to appear strong or to evade the truth of our feelings. When fear warns us of danger, it's summarizing all the information being received by the five senses. Fear calls our attention to a possible threat to our well-being. (Viscott, 1976, p. 54)

Another way to move beyond fear is to stop honoring it through our behavior and choice. This step is relevant only when we *know* it is in our best interest to act against our fears. In this case, as we accept that we are human enough to be fearful, we slowly and simultaneously continue along our previously chosen path, *as if* fear had no hold on us. A bright corporate executive's comments help us see what this might be like:

I really like not being married. But sometimes I get frightened about this truly conscious choice. I mean, what would I do if I got cancer? Whom do I have and whom could I lean on? Yet, there is something within me that puts this concern aside. I don't suppress it, but I don't do anything about it, either. That's why I consider this one of my best choices. I haven't given in to my nameless worries.

I choose consistently for what my best self truly needs: independence, privacy and a lack of someone else's judgment about my life. I felt strong and capable when I realized I've had enough courage to choose for myself in this way. I'm truly glad about the directions I've taken.

SELF-ACCEPTANCE AS A LIFE-CHOICE

As we move beyond our fear, we touch our own power. This comes in spurts. Indeed, much power seems to accompany self-acceptance. We then have the strength to make life-choices with more potency—without fretting, holding ourselves back, apologizing or in other ways doing ourselves in. When we have thought sufficiently through a problem, or grown as persons, so that fear is not our prime motivator, we realize that our "right" choices are often easy, unpressured, our goals quite reachable. As one man said:

> I used to think that the goals I had were impossible dreams, but as I grew in self-esteem and courage, I learned these impossibles were only the goals that *others* had for me.

> The things I really desired were simple for me to attain— they just flowed. Yet they required arduous work and patience. In time and with patience, as I applied myself, the activities I put myself to wholeheartedly began to feel natural and easy.

Another person also spoke of the value of learning to listen to himself. He said that everything he'd ever done well had been accomplished "without the voice in the head—that is, without inner criticism or subvocalization. When I trusted my inner sense I have done things I never believed I could do."

When we put ourselves under the influence of a courageous, life-giving spirit, then we are able to make decisions that move us away from what I call "consensus reality"—that is, the popular wisdom or collective expectations for our lives. This makes it easier to embrace ourselves *as we are*, validating ourselves as the unique person we are within ourselves. Self-acceptance is a key, critical factor in moving beyond fear.

When, on the other hand, we live our life out of the rules or mindset of others, it is hard to know where their standards, measures for right and wrong, value systems and ambitions leave off and our own begin. As the people quoted above have stated, when they allowed themselves to listen to what they *knew* within, they lived fulfillingly.

But such knowing, as well as the strength to act upon it, is only made possible as we have the inner silence and self-support to *hear* what we need. As we listen to ourselves deeply enough to recognize what will bring life to us, we learn, just as significantly, to recognize what will kill us.

This life/death issue is a slippery one: it is sometimes hard to put a finger on just exactly what we need for greater life and to separate this from choices that will mean the end of us. Some goals we set for ourselves are created out of our childhood frame of reference, which kept us in bondage to the opinions of others. Choosing from this reference point can cause the death of all that is fine, sweet and perfectible in us.

A person who had grown up in a home with a schizophrenic mother had a dream in which this truth was illustrated as only a dream can do it:

> In my dream I am supposed to lecture to a group of business people about the problems children have when they grow up in homes where there is mental illness. In order to prepare for the speech, I must first research this matter. In my readings I discover that when children live through such experiences, they put their "dead selves" into their life with their parents, into their early experiences, and they preserve their living selves somewhere deep within themselves. This is how they survive.

This dream holds a powerful secret: there is an "inner man, a hidden man of the heart," to use biblical language, whom we keep down in order to live out the desires of our worldly self. The unveiling of our inner person may be the only real work and purpose of our life. Whatever outer vocations we might utilize to bring ourselves into being as *living* persons, whatever outer supports, symbols or techniques we lean on to help us become whole beings, we must stop choosing as if we were lifeless entities. Only when we complete this work do our choices thereafter have potency, flow from us, become almost effortless. This "flow" is certain, even when our choices involve a loss or an inner struggle.

On the other side of our best choices, we feel cleaner, more honest, more at peace within ourselves. Once we begin a momentum of this sort, we need no coaxing, forcing or directing from any external law, book, or person to choose healthfully—such is the power of this life-force within us to move us when we open to it. In fact, there seems to be an ironic twist here: these decisions, the ones designed to bring out our best and highest self, are often the ones people around us (family or friends or the various institutions to which we pay homage in daily life) counsel us against. One man, a former priest, put it this way:

> Leaving the Jesuits ten years after I joined them was a time of great turmoil for me. While I knew in my *heart* that I was right to leave, it took my *head* six months to come around. It was very hard figuring out what I needed to do for me when so many were advising me I "should" do the opposite—that is, stay.

Another person spoke of a similar experience. In her case, she contemplated a divorce for over ten years, while her family and friends advised against it. Her husband agreed that they should separate; the marriage had been a mistaken commitment from the start for both parties. Out of loyalty and friendship to one another, out of a sense of social responsibility to the institution of marriage and their community, they stayed married.

When we finally realized we had betrayed ourselves, that each of us had a truer life to lead outside the bounds of our marriage, that our earlier vows—made, actually when we were just children—were mistaken ones, we had to go against everyone's advice and counsel. But we made the choice to terminate our marriage, and since that time have moved along much more honorable paths.

I respect myself a whole lot more since standing up to the truth of my experience. In an odd and ironic sort of way, my former husband and I love one another more now, with a purity and deeper quality of commitment, than when we were pretending to be happily married.

Each of these persons' stories, and especially that of the person who dreamed we put our "dead selves" into our early life experiences, reminds me of Christ's teachings about that part in us who is a murderer—from the beginning we are its children. From the start there is in us a spirit that hates the truth, hates the light, hates us.

Increasingly, as I observe myself *un*doing damages from my previous decisions, as I interview and listen to people talk about their *un*doing corrective work, I have come to believe that many of our earlier decisions and major life-choices (e.g., career, marriage, whether to have or not to have children, etc.) are made out of our "dead selves"; from the ground of being of self-loathing and the wish to die. Part of full personhood is to so precisely attend to ourselves inwardly that we "hear" what our life-giving self needs and wants in order to be born anew. We can do ourselves great service by simply noticing whether our daily choices are life-supporting or not.

An actor told of his struggle to find a way to express his living self.

I have always loved my father and always wished him to be proud of me. Because he is a sports-enthusiast, I tried football in my teens. This was so hard for me—I'm just not good at sports, especially not a rough sport like football. I experienced all sorts of stress, injuries and failure. I had to push myself into every game. But it didn't work for me.

My dad also loved the theater. He actually wanted to be an actor himself. When I went out for high school drama club and got a part, I noticed how easy it was for me. It was fun. There was no efforting to it, although I worked very hard. I was good at it and I knew it. That was the best part—that I knew myself to be good at something I enjoyed. So I've stayed on.

Maybe the things we're supposed to do are actually the easy things for us. Flow—not force—may be the order of all successful lives.

Indeed, as this man says, for this interior self to have its rebirth, no force is necessary: whether by means of a grace, or simply by our natural/healthy unfolding as we develop along the lines of this truest self, we are reborn, made a "new man." Then we are able to live increasingly in spontaneous obedience to our living self. No contemporary writer speaks of this more eloquently than Thomas Merton:

The law of our life can be summed up in the axiom "be what you are." . . . The spontaneity of this inner "law" is like the organic law governing the growth of a flower or of a tree. When St. Paul talks about the "fruits of the Spirit," his metaphor suggests something of the way in which a tree brings forth flowers and fruits without instruction, without command, without help from anyone. (Merton, 1961, p. 237)

Despite such ease and spontaneity, for many reasons most often a battle ensues as we attempt to move in the direction of our true life—as if we stir up sleeping dragons as we come to life. Probably the battle ensues because we live amongst a lie: it lives within us, and around us, and gives rise to our unbelief. What we "stir up" is no doubt what Scripture terms "principalities of darkness."

Perhaps this is at least in part what is meant by taking up our cross: that both symbolically and concretely, dying on the cross (as well as the rebirth that follows) is an *actual* event. If we want to live out our intrinsically good nature, the multiple small deaths that we go through along the way are requisite deaths: ego-deaths, deaths of our self-will, deaths as we relinquish the world's symbols of success, status and security, the dying of the murderer within—all these are experienced in order to move beyond fear.

These notions of dying on the cross, or entering a reborn state, or traversing the darkest of nights so as to find our way home, are not original ideas. These have been written about extensively by poets and mystics and saints. In terms of death, this *is* both a mystic death and an actual one. In terms of new life, this is both a mystic coming-to-life and an actual rebirth. We are both symbolically dying to our old self (with all the ways, values, habits and mistaken notions of that old self) as well as experiencing a concrete, practical death of sorts, with its material, this-world consequences, inconveniences and letting-gos that must be endured to so change ourselves that we relate in a transformed way to the world around us.

The mystic Jacob Boehme described the cross as a symbol of regeneration and initiation. The cross represents external, worldly life; the crown of thorns represents the suffering of the soul within our physical body; the figure nailed to the cross "symbolizes the death and surrender of the self-will." (Hartman, 1929, p. 326)

Boehme, too, considered humans as having within them "two" persons, the holy and the external one:

> The holy and heavenly man, hidden in the [external] man, is as much in heaven as God and heaven is in him, and the heart or light of God is begotten and born in him . . . the true man, regenerated and new-born in Christ is not in this world . . . and although he is in the body, nevertheless he is in God. (Ibid., p. 327)

Within this sphere of development, there arrives the matter of facing and accepting our dark side. This, and I want to emphasize this point, is different to me than what I referred to earlier as our "dead self." We might view our dark side as that aspect of ourselves which we try to keep out of sight, our Prodigal Son, as it were. Unconventional, tender-hearted, vulnerable, impulsive, quirky, this is uniquely "us," even though seemingly flawed in some embarrassing way. On the other hand, the "dead self" might be thought of as life-draining, as striving for perfection, living only for its own flawless idealization. This spirit has a killing nature. Under its spell, we live for ourselves alone, love ourselves alone (with a narcissism which finally is our undoing). This aspect-of-self often is the force behind our self-defeating, early life choices.

Our dark side, however, is as vital a part of our real self as is our brighter, socially-acceptable self—more perhaps. Although we hide this part because we feel it to be, in this respect, quite shameful, our "dark self" may not motivate us toward self-annihilation. Quite the opposite. This is the fully-human self, the creative self, the innocent, guileless self. It may have been what the Transcendental poet Walt Whitman referred to as "the Other I am."

Carl Jung called this dark side "the shadow within," and wrote often on this subject, saying that in the course of our lifetime, we are somehow healed by accepting our imperfections. Moreover, we are punished (by sickness, misfortune, or a lack of vitality) if we try to hide our shortcomings, either from ourselves or others.

> There appears to be a conscience in mankind which severely punishes the man who does not and at some time, at whatever cost to his pride, cease to defend and assert himself, and instead confess himself fallible and human. Until he can do this, an impenetrable wall shuts him out from the living experience of feeling himself a man among men. (Jung, 1933, p. 35)

Our major life-choices give us the chance to acknowledge what we truly are, as both positive and blemished persons, and thus join the "living experience" of being fully human. A friend of mine, a priest, shared his story with me.

> A significant life-choice involved my consciously recognizing and accepting my being gay. Not only accepting, but rejoicing in this being a God-given gift to me. Paradoxically this has happened while not being sexually active—I have kept a vow of celibacy. This decision was a long, unclear decision, based on my being increasingly unhappy with myself. Eventually I learned that I was acceptable as I am, and learned that I could not be dishonest.

> This meant I had to overcome a vast amount of emotional pressure put on me by family and society about being "evil." The end result has been considerable happiness with myself, discovering new depths within, and I think discovering a gift to recognize some of the pressures others might be living with themselves. Further, my self-acceptance has brought me an ever deepening respect for the quality of honesty that has affected most positively all of my life.

His willingness to accept himself *as he is* (instead of forcing himself to be what he *wishes* to be or what he feels others want him to be) is the elegant choice. This is the choice that has brought him "an ever-deepening respect for the quality of honesty" in himself. It is not either his being or not being gay that heals. Truth is the healer. The fact that he demonstrates toward himself, eventually toward others, the highest truth and that quality of love that heals, makes him whole. It was Martin Buber who taught that in the realm of our human lives, the influence of spirit is found through "faithful courage and faithful love."

These agents of spirit, Buber wrote, appear in more than just thought and theory: they exert their influence on us, on our lives and actions and on our choices. Truthfulness, courage and faithful love are what my friend chose to demonstrate when he consciously recognized and accepted his particular sexual inclination. This choice—not this or that sexual preference—moved him closer into right relationship with his true self.

By loving himself enough to live a truthful life, he joins the living experience of full humanness wherein each of us is imperfect in some way. Our pretenses to the contrary keep us apart from living as fully human; not only our fears separate us from a rich life. Of course if we are crippled and thwarted by massive fear, here too we cannot live as humans must. But our social pretenses, our strivings to conform to external gods, to be like others, our desperate need to fit in, are all ways that we fragment ourselves inwardly and cut ourselves off from the human experience. Yet, each time we choose in a way that rights a previous wrong, straightens out some crookedness or dishonesty within, we come a step closer to mending our fragmented self. Thus we move a step closer to a fully human life. A film I once saw had a line in it that said something like this:

> When people say they're only human it's usually because
> they've been acting like a beast.

Now, by "fully human" I do not mean "only human" in
the sense that we give ourselves an excuse for all our shortcomings and base, impoverished choices. I mean fully human so
that we self-affirmingly cease pretending that we are what we
are not, so that we join the human community by accepting
our natural gifts and the full range of emotions and traits avail-
able to us. But I also mean that being fully human allows us to
accept our spiritual side, lets us know we can reach spiritual
heights—peaks of self-understanding and supernatural self-
realization—as easily as any other person. Ironically, these
peaks come to us at the precise moment we are willing to drop
our false approaches and defenses to life.

In his wonderful book, *How To Have a Lifestyle*, Quentin
Crisp talks about the need to journey to our interior world if
we would size up our assets and our flaws—or as Crisp puts it,
"what your friends call 'the trouble with you' " (Crisp, 1979).
The purpose of this journey is to reconcile our glamorized self-
evaluation with the awful things others may say or think about
us. Reconciliation is easier in the light of self-acceptance. If we
know ourselves to be inflexible, overly sensitive, dull-witted or
whatever, then we might just as well accept that and get on
with our lives with the certainty that on the other side of accepting that inglorious trait will be some loosening of it and
even perhaps a positive use for that trait. For example, the inflexible person may be an artist or a precise scientist who tol-
erates no deviation from standards he or she holds to be
excellent. The sensitive person who suffers inordinately when
tasteless jokes are made about others may, on the other side of
this, be an intuitive genius in interpersonal matters. As long as
"the trouble with us" is only a problem to others, perhaps we
need not do much about it. Crisp puts it this way:

If, when you peer into your soul, you find that you are ordinary, then ordinary is what you must remain, but you must be so ordinary that you can imagine someone saying, "Come to my party and bring your humdrum friend," and everyone knowing that he meant you. (Ibid., p. 48)

When we know ourselves, as we accept what we know as "the truth" of us, our choices become much easier—even the difficult ones. One woman said this of her process for tackling life's problems:

I am guided always and ultimately by my heart, my deeper needs and feelings. Often this is contrary to what my head says or to what seems logical. But I know from experience that this is where real satisfaction lies, so I choose in that direction even if it is contrary to my intellect's advice.

Whatever our choices, when we are in touch with our best instincts and impulses, life works as it should. Even mistakes iron themselves out quickly. Recently, for example, I received a phone call from a service-business offering to handle some of my firm's activities. I did not like the voice on the other end of the phone. But my intellect told me I needed this service. Within forty-eight hours the caller and I had signed and then, almost as quickly, cancelled a contract. The signing of the contract was followed by an abrupt, heated communication between the two of us, during which I felt it would be fruitless to continue with our original agreement. The point is this: had I initially listened to my own interior hunch, I could have spared myself—as well as the other person—the time lost in negotiations. The point is *also* that, because I know what I need and want in terms of working relationships with others, I was able to exit the contract easily and forthrightly.

When we are integrated as persons, when all the sub-selves and various parts of ourselves become harmonized, then our choice-making flows. Then our choices have an integrity and a spontaneity that let us know very quickly what we require for life to function effectively. Somehow a dialogue develops between our self and the deeper parts of ourselves that naturally brings us into contact with "knowing" what we must do in a matter. In the case I just mentioned, the woman on the other end of the phone was outraged that I was not more flexible about one of the points she wanted in the contract, namely the starting date. She scolded me for not accepting her input. Knowing myself as I do, I know full well that I am not particularly flexible on matters relating to my firm. Even more importantly, I have stopped "trying" to be something I am not. The lovely thing about such self-acceptance, as audacious as it might seem at face value, is that I also accept that some people are not going to enjoy working with me. They are not "wrong" for not liking to work with me. I am not "wrong" for being the way I am.

This is another way that self-acceptance empowers us: when we know and accept what we are, we can get on with our lives, adjusting ourselves when we must, adjusting our sometimes-idealized goals when we must, so that our real self, the living self within us, has the power to live itself out in our everyday affairs.

My example also brings up another benefit of self-acceptance: when we accept ourselves for what we are, we do not blame ourselves for our faulty choices. After all, no one is perfect. We are human. The point of all self-development work, and the point of this discussion, is to help us become *more* human. That may mean becoming more imperfect, but humanly so, in such a way that we forgive ourselves for our imperfect choices and flawed ways of being. Along with that, we are better able to forgive others for their mistakes and imperfections. Thus, we love ourselves and others with a higher quality love, a more compassionate love, and even need one another to a greater degree. This is not to suggest we stop trying to improve ourselves but that we modify our idealized image of ourselves as godlike.

If I know myself to be inflexible about certain things, then I know I must surround myself with others who have the flexibility, candor and maturity to help me in this area. If I know myself to be one way or another, then I know I need the other for his or her strength and virtue to offset my weakness. Thus we are both served.

As we grow in self-acceptance, we face an intriguing, but also frustrating, irony: as we become healthier, we sometimes feel less so, especially at first. What is actually happening is that we are becoming more aware of what we do to get in our own way.

One corporate executive I worked with, known for his extremely stressful responses and his abrasive over-controlling manner, began a meditation program upon my recommendation. In a matter of weeks he realized that as he got into his car in the morning to drive to work, he began to feel anxious. "I feel a surge of fear within myself. I feel this surge coming on as I get into the car." After a short discussion, he realized that he kept himself motivated by scaring himself in this way. But, more important, he knew he could now correct himself because of his increased awareness on the whole matter.

> I am more sensitive to what is occurring within my body. Now as I *feel* the fear, I can choose to redirect this energy by changing my thoughts and habits. In the past I was unconscious about what I was doing to myself. My growth in awareness seems a sign that I am changing.

With added self-acceptance came release of his outworn, destructive habit of frightening himself into production. The love he felt for himself enhanced his life, and also enhanced the lives of others with whom he had contact.

Another man, recently promoted to a highly visible and pressured job, also returned to a previous "bad habit." He began sleeping excessively. After consulting a physician, who said there was no physical reason for his sleepiness, he worked with a therapist. Over time he realized that he had slipped into a childhood habit of taking naps whenever he was afraid, as a way of hiding from his problems. He also realized that by becoming more assertive, he would be able to give up the old habit pattern.

When we enter periods of rapid growth and change, it is natural to regress, to revert back to old fears, habits or unproductive behaviors. Some people lose weight when they are anxious; others gain weight. Some sleep fitfully; others can't sleep at all, or sleep too much. These are all ways people unconsciously protect themselves against the unfamiliar.

For more serious, self-destructive behaviors, therapy may be in order. For the milder "bad" habits, self-help may be curative. The healthier we are, the more able we are to understand these cycles of behavior and to tolerate such "imperfection" or backsliding in ourselves, even as we seek help from professionals who can guide us through the trauma or change. The more neurotic we are, the greater likelihood we will hold up an idealized, impossible-to-reach standard for our behavior and measure ourselves rigidly against that. We will berate ourselves cruelly when we fall the tiniest bit short. We punish ourselves for being human instead of reflecting a more human attitude for ourselves during a time of struggle and learning.

Woody Allen, with typical wry humor, spoke in an interview about the value that obsessing about small things had for him:

I've always felt that if one can arrange one's life so that one can obsess about small things, it keeps you from obsessing about the really big things. If you obsess about the big things you are impotent and frightened because there is nothing you can do about aging and death. But the little things you can spend days obsessing about, such as a good punch line for the third act. And this is a nice problem to obsess over, because it's not surgery. . . . I'm a little more morbid than the average person. (Allen, *Rolling Stone*, April 9, 1987, issue 487, p. 40)

Although I'm not suggesting that we substitute small negative habits for larger ones, it is probably our human nature to do just that. Not insignificant to this discussion is the gentle humor Allen possesses about his own foibles. Comedy, for him, diffuses the harsh glare of our pain, unfulfilled yearnings and excessive worry. This, it seems to me, is a hallmark of health and simple good sense. Our habits and idiosyncrasies have a funny overtone; this humor is also part and parcel of a well-lived life. It is essential that we keep our humor and our patience as we progress toward self-acceptance—especially at first, perhaps, when our faults and flaws may seem so glaringly obvious to us. Learning to laugh at, or with, our dark side is another way to move beyond fear.

THE FLOW OF OUR CHOICE-MAKING

In talking about their progression toward self-acceptance, many people mention how their choices began to flow, once they learned to listen to themselves. As the young football player-turned-actor said: "Flow, not force, may be the order of successful lives."

As self-knowledge and self-acceptance increase, our own

insights start to work in our behalf. We simply "know" what we need to do. It is this knowing that makes our choices begin to flow more effortlessly for us.

One woman had been worrying for years about whether to end an unhappy marriage. She argued back and forth with herself, and always ended her inner-dialogue feeling more confused. One weekend the solution fell clearly into place for her:

> I was driving home from the desert where I'd spent the weekend in seclusion. Typically, I'd fretted about my predicament. That's the way I habitually spent time. As I drove around a particularly lovely mountain range, its ridges soft pink against the morning light, I *knew* what I needed to do: it was so absurdly simple.

> After that, I just enacted the scenario that had come to me during the drive home. I ended my marriage. Just like that. It was over. As it turned out—and this amazed me— my husband was not hurt. He was not surprised. He was relieved! He'd been stewing about the same thing. He was lonely. And he wanted out, too.

Our intuition sparks such "Aha!" experiences, such as this woman describes. Still, we must remember that our development can take a long time. These healthy choices may flow from our insights, but they put rigorous demands on us. That is what takes time: we are not ready, psychically speaking, to choose and live our way into the realization we have had. The sum total of our realizations, and the subsequent choices made out of our newly gained understanding, show us what we need to do. The healthier we grow, the more mature our development, the less confused we are about what to do in our lives or about how to do it. Clarity and order begin to reign. As with the woman cited above, our insights introduce years of choices and changes that will also lay the groundwork for further enhanced growth. A positive cycle is inevitably put into place.

This brings up another aspect about flow in choice-making. As we lay a groundwork for healthy choices (letting our choices flow from us rather than forcing them) we also open the way for a hierarchy of "right" choices. To say this another way, life-supporting or productive choices emerge from our past choices which are themselves productive.

Small choices that we make in our day-to-day lives lead up, incrementally, to larger life-choices. With each positive, life-supportive choice we consciously make, we feel more *capable* when dealing with the next one. The flow of our choice-making builds because our world-view and new sense of what is important shapes what we do in each instance of our lives.

A friend of mine, an artist and writer, tells me she no longer makes choices per se.

> I almost never decide what to do. I do what I can do. If there are several possibilities (there rarely are; it is usually *this* or *not this*), I do what fits in with my current momentum. I have stopped wanting certain "things" to happen or turn out the way I want them to. I let events determine their own course, and only when I am forced by others or events to act, do I do what I can at that time with the energy I have in that phase, with the commitments I want to keep. If I later have cause to regret a decision, I don't. I know that I made my choices under certain conditions that caused me to do what I did.

> If later under new conditions, I see where I could have saved myself time, trouble or heartache correcting the original situation (like a marriage that no longer fits), I am free to do it without condemning myself for the first decision. I did the best I could under the circumstances of

where I was, developmentally, at the time or with the information I had at the time.

I guess I see myself like a train. I am set on a track: I go
where I can, at the speed I can as long as I can. If a barrier—my body or someone to whom I listen—says stop, I
see if I can. If I can, O.K.; if I can't, then others will have
to remake some of their decisions.

She went on to say that for her, choice-making is now a
part of how she sees life, how she relates to herself and others.
Larger choices are a result of the tiny decisions she makes
everyday. These add up to be the day itself; each day adds up
to be a month and so on.

My children are visiting me. Their children are with them,
so there's a lot of rock music being played loudly around
our home. I had a choice to make this morning: did I want
to send them off to a picnic so that I could sit quietly by
myself and read Virginia Woolf, or did I want to entertain
them here all day and listen to that blaring hard rock? I
chose to send them off to have a picnic and spend the day
quietly reading. This seems to be the way I choose these
days—it comes out of what I want for my life. These insignificant decisions add up so that the big choices are
more or less handled by the way I live.

Another example of this type of choice-making: we both
had been invited to a book-signing party and writing seminar.
I decided not to go, but didn't know my friend had been invited, nor was I aware she also declined. My decision not to go
was based on the fact that I prefer to write whenever I have a
chance. The autographing would have deprived me of the opportunity to write this chapter. I am more motivated to write

than to do almost anything else. My friend described her choice in much lovelier terms:

> I thought about going. Then I looked at the person who was presenting the writing seminar, how he handles the material, what he writes, what he's about, his philosophy of marketing books and so on. I saw that we were on completely different paths, so I asked myself what possible links could there be between his path and mine? I saw that there was virtually nothing I could gain from going, so I stayed home to work on my own projects. That's the kind of little choice that adds up into a way of living life.

6

A Fighting Spirit
Till the End

Rage, rage against the dying of the light.

Dylan Thomas

Those who live vigorously, meaningfully and even attractively until a ripe old age demonstrate many of the values of wholeness, or adult actualization. I would go so far as to say one cannot live well or fulfill one's life as one ages unless one also moves toward actualization. The characteristics of creativity, continued adult growth, autonomy and elegant choice-making show up again and again in old people who remain vital in their last years. A starting question for us at this point is *why?* Why do some people age well while some—perhaps the majority—still travel along a path of aging that leads to a frail, demoralized state of being?

This question is important because more and more of us are getting older all the time. For the first time, as of this writing, America has reached zero population growth. Because of our low national birth rate, persons sixty-five and older now outnumber teenagers. The fastest growing segment in our population is the over-eighty-five group. While there are now 35,000 people who are one hundred years of age, that number will triple by the year 2000.

The aging trend has begun to affect consumer, voting and

life-style patterns; this trend predictably will continue with advances in medicine and geriatric research. Schools, the media, medical institutions—such as hospitals and university research centers—will probably focus increasingly on ways to enhance life during all its stages: childhood, young adult, mid-adult and old age. As we live longer we will, collectively, ask ourselves what it will take to live productively until "the end."

BREAKING THROUGH RESTRICTIONS

In his wonderfully instructive book titled *The View From 80*, author Malcolm Cowley (writing when he was in his ninth decade) tells us that the body imposes its own brand of restrictions on us as we age. Its primary and constant message is "You are old." It embellishes this idea with countless reminders on countless occasions. For example, using Cowley's list:

- When we notice that what we once did quickly, and from instinct, we must do step-by-step and with much forethought;
- When our bones and muscles ache or our eyes won't focus;
- When we can't stand on one foot long enough to put on our trousers or our hosiery;
- When we see more and more little bottles of pills in our medicine cabinet;
- When it takes longer to do everything. (Cowley, 1980)

One way of combating our body's limits is to continue physical activity—especially when we don't feel up to it. This is precisely what those who age productively are most likely to do. This is one of those types of choices that, to my way of seeing things, is more elegant but which, also, may be the harder choice. In order to live with distinction and grace, one simply must push on.

Cowley interviewed only those who were over eighty for his book. Persons who refused to give in to the body's message of "you are old" were the more robust ones. One man, age eighty-six, said that he continued doing the physical work that he had always done:

> At seven this morning, I did what I've been doing for the last 15 years, ever since I had to slow down. When I opened my eyes I did my 20 sit-ups while still on my back, jumped out of bed, slipped into my swim trunks, did the very same calisthenics we did in the army when Pershing went after Pancho Villa in 1916. (Cowley, 1980, p. xi)

In *Growing Old Is Not for Sissies*, an inspiring book about senior athletes, author and photographer Etta Clark talks about her own shock when she, at forty, looked into the mirror and noticed an older woman squinting back. From then on, she grew more and more fascinated with the subject of healthy aging, and specifically with people who seem able to push back the clock. She found a small band of people over sixty who escaped age's frail and sickly destination. While on a magazine assignment, Clark met a man whose rugged image captured her imagination:

> I was doing a feature on [Joe Bruno's] 49th crossing of San Francisco's treacherous Golden Gate, a mile-long swim in icy water and unpredictable tides. This was no soft sympathy piece on a curious old man paddling in the bay. It was a story about a real athlete competing in a tough sport, a guy who reaches for his limits. (Clark, 1986, p. vii)

His example led Clark to photograph others who, like him, were also doggedly determined to confront the physical limits of age. She introduces us to such people as a ninety-four year old woman who has just had cataract surgery, yet who is already practicing her golf swing in her yard, preparing to return as quickly as possible to the links as the champion golfer she is. We meet Sister Marion Irvine (only fifty-six) who, at forty-eight—for the first time in her life—started jogging and who, five months later, entered an eight-mile competitive run. She placed fourth among all women entrants. Five years later she became the oldest woman ever to qualify for the Olympic Trials in track and field.

Another senior athlete was the oldest man ever to complete the Hawaiian Iron Man Triathelon: 1¼ mile swim, 128 mile bike ride and 26.2 mile run. He accomplished this when he was seventy-four. His motto, "Rest makes rust," may be good choice-making advice for us all, but especially as we age.

Anyone who keeps up on medical news at all knows that moderate exercise has been found to help all sorts of ills. Regular physical exercise has been shown to lower the incidence of stress-related illnesses and to help alleviate depression. Some psychiatrists no longer will treat depressed persons without a commitment on the patient's part to participate in some type of disciplined sport. Such sports as brisk walking, swimming, yoga or even the mildest aerobics can be done throughout life. These can be started at almost any age, with a doctor's approval. These sports help circulation, improve the cardiovascular system, move oxygen through the body—to our brains and hearts and legs and eyes—and improve our spirits.

It is primarily this last benefit that interests me. Hope and optimism are required daily to combat and counteract our body's "You Are Old" slogan. In our youth-oriented society, there is still another reason for getting all the hope and optimism we can: namely our society, our friends and family, and the media all send us that "You are old" message—but in more subtle ways. Recently, on an airplane trip, I overheard the flight attendant speaking to an elderly woman. She used a tone most of us would find irritating, even if overhearing someone talk to a pet or infant: cloying, patronizing, superior. The elderly passenger noticed, for she said something to her own seat partner. But she rode along in quiet dignity, and said nothing to the airline attendant. After all, what can one say in such a situation?

At other times, in other places, I observe people in a hurry almost knock down older people who aren't walking as quickly, then getting angry at them for moving slowly. I have shown such irritation myself. In the face of such slights, living in a society that devalues people as they age, we must have hope and inner resolve to keep going—even when our body and other people tell us we might not make it.

A friend doing research on Haiku received a letter from an eighty year old Japanese poet. The poet said that staying young was a matter of mind and body, but that it was easier to *feel* young when others saw us in a youthful light:

> As you may understand, youth in mind and body is needed for composing Haiku. When someone says that I am very young for my age, I feel very happy, as if I were refreshed by the sunlight and sea wind at my hometown open to the Pacific.

Such inspiring older persons are active all their lives. They "die with their boots on," to use a phrase I've heard some lawyers use to describe how they intend to age. They do not see themselves someday retiring, but rather reinterpreting their professional involvement in a way that will allow them to continue working even after they cease taking on new clients or heavy case loads.

Most importantly, vital older persons persevere as learners: they study, they are open to learning—"lifelong learning" as U.C.L.A. has termed it—and are helpful to future generations, to others, as long as humanly possible. These people flourish despite the message from their bodies and society that they are old. Their greatest message to us lies in their daily life. It is as if their fighting spirit moves them through and beyond the trials of age. This fighting spirit is behind their choices, as it is behind our own elegant choices, even when younger. This tenacity, this holding of one's ground, this persevering life-force, is what I call elegant.

MEANINGFUL WORK AND PROJECTS

When I am with older persons who inspire me, I notice that their lives are marked by purposeful activity—not simply busy-work or aimless, superficial hobbies. They participate fully in projects, work or community affairs. They invest their energies and talents so as to benefit themselves and others. Earlier, especially in my first book *Ordinary People as Monks and Mystics* on self-actualizing adults, I explored that quality in actualizing persons that I call "the stewardship pattern."

Older persons, thriving until their last days, are excellent stewards. As a steward, the individual gives something back to future generations, a behavioral pattern psychiatrist Erik Erikson termed "generativity." And in so doing, they themselves gain hope, energy and zest for living. They continue to feel needed, because they *are* needed. They continue to feel they belong because they do—to a circle of friends and colleagues who care about them. They find meaning and purpose in their lives—not just by doing something that gives them pleasure (and it is important to note that their projects do provide intrinsic pleasure), but by working in a way that enlarges their world, provides a real service, expands them continually as persons.

The author, educator and political activist Helen Nearing, who (with her husband Scott) for more than fifty years grew her own food, cut her own wood, promoted the virtues of natural living and robust health, serves as an illustration of this sort of purposefulness. Helen and Scott Nearing traveled and lectured widely. Although Scott died recently, Helen is still involved in the work they started in their youth. In a recent article, she said:

> I feel pretty close to the end. There's nothing wrong with me physically. I'm perfectly healthy and well. I feel that if there is something left for me to contribute, I'll still contribute, and then I'll go on myself and see what's doing over there. (Costas, 1986, p. 60)

To her, the essence of the good life is summed up in her philosophy: "To grow, to learn, to experience, to contribute, to share, to be intensely in the moment in which you are living, to get the most out of everything that happens to you and to realize that we are all here to contribute and share." (Ibid.)

Nearing sounds much like the senior athlete whose motto was "Rest makes rust." While some older people are active as athletes, others are politically active or diligent scholars or gardeners. A correspondent, of about sixty, replied to my bid for choice-making advice for younger people with this suggestion:

> I have no advice to offer. Rather I would share my experience for what it is worth: I have never stopped seeking to learn, the more the better. The best way I have found to learn is through the explorations of play. I use a process for decision-making that I seem to have known and understood all my life. It is also good for problem-solving and conflict resolution—I call it play. Play, play, play.

Whether one learns through reading, through study groups, through one's involvement with a lifelong interest in a particular project, or through playing seems less important than staying open to the learning and growth process itself. By continuing to be creative and contributive as human beings, we stay alive. The point is *to continue.* To do so often takes a fighting spirit, because it is so tempting to quit when we're tired, discouraged or sick.

If our choices, each and every day, are made with just a bit of this spirit, if we see ourselves obstinately staying with it, we will be better for it. Of course, there is no rule for this and—as someone in my forties—I am hardly qualified to give advice to those twice my age. But, at my point in life, that is how I see it.

CREATIVITY IN OLD AGE

A friend of mine, professor and poet Thom Tammaro, co-produced an anthology of poetry written by elder poets: poets over the age of sixty-five. As an example of the type of involvement and spirit I am describing, one of the poets, James Broughton, wrote these lines on his sixty-fifth birthday:

I am an old boy glowing as the light fades
I have a new childhood ready for the dusk
    I drop kick the sunset
    I polevault to sundown
I perish rightly on my nonstop dayshift.
                (Tammaro, Koontz, 1981)

As the poets in Tammaro's anthology demonstrate, creativity does not dim with age. And it may be, ultimately, *the* way to deal with the perils of aging, be these physical or mental.

Creativity, however it is expressed, is the solution—perhaps the only solution—for dealing with *any* life problem, loss, anger or disappointment. The fears, losses or frustrations of existence can be resolved, transcended and spoken about with a triumphant voice *if and when* we find creative outlets for these often trapped or confusing emotions. When we create something, we destroy the negative power that has stored itself in us as disease, disorganization or unhappiness. Somehow, through our creative acts we draw negativity out of ourselves and are enlarged as persons, more able than before as individuals. In short, we build life over death. We honor life—not death—through our creative actions.

The Names Project Quilt, designed to internationally honor those who've died from AIDS, is an example of creative endeavor on a mass scale. In this project, family and friends of the deceased designed and then sewed together individual patches of quilts, one panel per person who died, to commemorate the lives of those who lost their lives to the disease. The Viet Nam Memorial Wall in Washington D.C. and the organization called M.A.D.D. (Mothers Against Drunk Drivers) are examples of wide-scale, national projects that creatively attempt to resolve deeply felt personal losses. When we, as individuals, give witness to some loss by writing a poem, a book or even in our personal journal, we also take steps to resolve our hurt. The hurt comes *out* of us, into the light, into humankind's shared body of knowledge or understanding, and we are relieved somewhat.

As we experience ourselves aging, we can also find this sort of relief if we can find and express ourselves through unique creative outlets. I believe creative persons, who always have a rich inner life, lead a qualitatively enhanced life, even when ill or economically strapped. Something in them, their inner person, lives in dignity despite any worldly setback. Perhaps this is what St. Paul meant when he said, talking about his life in Christ, that although his outer man was getting older, the inner man was strong. People who are creative are usually spiritually inclined (although they might not be religious, per se) and may have an advantage in age because spiritual realities *do* grow more profound with time.

Spiritual persons of all ages, for example, understand the power of prayer and meditation. One technique, that of meditating upon a phrase of Scripture, shows how *increased* time benefits the person. After using this technique for a time—as the phrase is digested, dissected, contemplated upon—it becomes us, it bolsters us, it makes us strong on the inside even though on the outside we may look and feel weak. Persons who study Scripture in this way are stronger within despite age, just as was the case with St. Paul.

Whether we are spiritual or not, creativity in age helps us give to future generations. This is true when older persons see that their time and energy is meeting the needs of the younger generation, or when they feel they are giving to "things that live on," as Cowley put it. He describes in his book how many older persons gardened, took care of animals or wrote books, and were revitalized by these acts. They knew their choices led to something that outlived their own individual lives. In this connection Cowley advises any aging person to think about the advantages of being creative:

> Artists in general have the strongest desire to fashion something whose life will be self-contained and independent of their own mortality. . . . But can't we all be artists, each in his own fashion? (Cowley, 1980, p. 70)

It is this creative drive that lets us exert our will, our energy and optimism to the very end of our days. As we cultivate our wholeness, we can each so easily be artists. Wholeness (or interior integration) and the creative process in our larger life are but one and the same thing: the whole life *is* the creative life, however it may appear to others.

There is simply no reason, save that of our own choices or the most grave, debilitating illness, why we cannot be creative up until the day we die. I have often quoted a favorite section of books by Norman Cousins in which he describes Pablo Casals on the eve of his ninetieth birthday. Casals was badly crippled with arthritis, but he continued to play the cello, becoming transformed by the activity:

> Twice in one day I had seen the miracle. A man almost 90, beset with the infirmities of old age, was able to cast off his afflictions, at least temporarily, because he knew he had something of overriding importance to do. . . . Creativity for Pablo Casals was the source of his own cortisone. It is doubtful whether any anti-inflammatory medication he would have taken would have been as powerful or as safe as the substances produced by the interaction of his mind and body. (Cousins, 1979, p. 74)

Cousins reports he himself was a man "energized by a torrential drive to use his mind and body." (Ibid.) Albert Schweitzer's work was healing in exactly the same way. Schweitzer believed that the most powerful prescription for any illness he had was his knowledge that he had a job to do. He once said,

> I have no intention of dying so long as I can do things. And if I do things, there is no need to die. So I will live a long, long time. (Cousins, Ibid., 80)

Schweitzer lived until he was ninety-five. He was essentially a person with purpose and creativity.

Whether we are possessed by such a drive seems less significant than that we choose, on a day-to-day basis—and here I am truly speaking about *each and every day*—to do the things that matter to us. All of us, regardless of age and socio-economic circumstance, can find a cause to pour our energies into. I have heard recently of prominent business executives who have given up all their position, power, and economic security to live in the streets with the homeless, simply because they want to help in a hands-on, direct manner. I have known people who were losing their sight and continued to create—even artists who had to hold their artwork so close to their faces in order to see that they were practically tasting the canvas. I've heard of musicians who practice every day, in spite of physical pain or a bone-deep fatigue that might cause lesser persons to put off practicing for another day. Not too long ago I read of a master bookbinder who was losing her vision because of cataracts, but who continued her artwork, and was even planning a trip to the Orient, prior to scheduling cataract surgery. She felt she had too much to do, all of it more important to her than a stay at the hospital. Another, a father of a friend, now ninety, was told thirty years ago that he should "take it easy," due to a bad heart. He left the doctor's office in a huff and has never gone back. He continues to live and play vigorously, spending his days investing in the stock market, playing tennis and bridge with friends. However and whatever it is each of us needs to do, the important thing is that we *keep on* doing it.

CREATIVITY AT ANY AGE

We must pay attention to our talents, to our creative drive and to strengthening our creativity muscles and individuality *all through* life so these will work for us as we age.

Creative people trust themselves. They trust themselves

to know what to do when there is no "blueprint" for their actions. They trust their brains and hearts to steer them correctly. They trust their intuitions more, for instance, than they trust a doctor's statistical probability that they will die. And they know that even if they are at their wit's ends about something, somehow they will figure out what to do. My sense is also that they are willing to die rather than abandon themselves through sheer distrust or self-discounting. There is a decided and well-researched link between high creativity and high self-esteem. So at any age, we can build our creative abilities by choosing in ways that help us trust ourselves more. The opportunities for such choices are limitless, but all revolve around the issue of our identifying what we need and want to do—and then doing just that.

Creative people of all ages are independent. One man, in his sixties, wrote to me about choice-making in his later years. He had this advice for younger people:

> The best teacher is yourself. No teacher can teach you anything, the learning has to go into you, and then you learn so that the truth of the idea is yours. It is essential that you understand the principles of a matter, and are able to *use* them so that it is not just words on a piece of paper, you will grasp ideas so they become your own knowledge. You will have the ability to use things, ideas and, yes, even people.

> Leadership [in our lives] is knowing the truth, explaining it, having it give back to you. . . . I say to kids, the truth will feed back and always sustain you in everything. Goodness feeds back; evil "sucks" your energy from you.

His lessons are those of a creative mind. Similarly, we heard earlier from a man who said he learned and solved life-problems by playing. Only those who are sufficiently well developed—as independent persons, as nonconformists, as leaders in their own lives—play with ideas or with knowledge in a way that enhances their total understanding and growth. I maintain that whole persons, and those moving toward wholeness, always create—even if only viable solutions to the problems of life.

Broken persons—the fragmented people who lack self-regard, those who discount their own perceptions while elevating the opinions and beliefs of others—cannot create. To create, at any age, we must have within us a touch of the rebel. This is because creation implies regrouping (or destruction) of data in a way that allows something totally new to be born.

If we allow ourselves to always choose in the safest way—and by this I mean in a way that has been adopted for us by others—we will never honor the real life in us. This is especially true as we age, because then it is harder to choose courageously. A recent television film, starring Kathryn Hepburn, depicted an older woman who wanted to marry a man younger than she and not of her faith. Although she was bright, sensitive and fully responsible as a widow with a large inheritance, her children wanted her to stay single. Or they wished she would marry someone in their social circle. But she was strong—strong enough to wear them down despite the pressure they exerted, no easy achievement considering she was in her eighties. This story ended happily only because Hepburn's character was tenacious and honored the life in herself. Unfortunately, if we avoid conflict, if we back away from confrontation on the small issues during our younger years, we have little clout on the larger issues when we age. Then not only will we lack creative drive, but we may very easily go along with what our children or society want "for our good"—even when we know, down deep, we are not well served by our choices. Therefore, early in life it is important to choose in ways that build our strength, courage and creative potential.

But we will not create anything, no matter how hard we try, if we are plagued with self-doubt or if we care too much about pleasing others. All our projects will then be developed with an eye toward what others think. Or we ourselves will think through a filter of the perceptions of people who are important to us. Creativity, as I'm discussing it here, is not just a "Sunday painting" activity. It is a way of being, which necessitates our becoming independent thinkers. This independence serves both our creative drive as well as that fighting spirit I talked about earlier. In a way, these may be one and the same. At the very least the muscles of our fighting spirit will have had some practice if we assert ourselves as independent persons. Then later in life we will have put our own internal equipment in place so that we can fight the battles of physical impairment, social rejection or self-rejection. Independence, high self-esteem, the willingness to think for ourselves, are all a part of the will to live. These enable us to fend for ourselves in old age.

DAILY CHOICES AND CREATIVITY

There are things we can do daily to stimulate our own creativity. Initially, especially if we have not considered ourselves in this light, we can begin our day by simple self-inquiry. We can ask ourselves what it is that we really want to do that day. The habit of self-inquiry, along the lines of our most meaningful and fulfilling activities, things we *enjoy*—rather than things we should do—will let us see what it is we "should" do that day. Then, of course, it is important to do those things as much as possible during the course of our lives.

We may notice that we have some self-correction to do. If we have never been comfortable doing what we most prefer, for instance, it may be necessary first to stop doing things we have habitually forced ourselves to schedule. We may realize we have to stop socializing in a certain manner. This was the case with one of my clients who, after his retirement, found that he hated going to lunch with his bridge-playing friends. Instead, he wanted to start a whole new pattern that would give him large chunks of time to work on his sculpting. But before he could do so, he had to stop his lunch meetings. This was hard for him to do. He felt he was rejecting his friends, but at the same time he felt that he needed an artistic outlet.

Regardless of our age, there is almost always some self-corrective work to be done. We all, sometimes, make "mistakes." Of mistakes, however, one older person wrote to me saying:

> There is no wrong, there is no mistake. Tune into your heart, you know all the answers.

As we "tune into our hearts" our creative answers come to us. Put another way, perhaps we become able to hear what is inside and what has been in us all along.

We also must correct ourselves on a daily basis, not simply examine the obvious big errors. The diaries of famous creative people show that they monitor their conduct, discipline themselves, are ever stretching towards standards of excellence. I always try to start small. In the safe areas of our life, the less significant areas, we can ask:

- Do I really want to do this? What do I truly need to do with my time today? After I do what I must do, what would appeal to me, help me be more enthused, rather than just worn out, at the end of the day?

- Can I say "No" to the things I find enervating? How can I practice this art so that I'm better able to use my time as I choose?

♦ What can I do today to learn something new? What ideas can I surround myself with—in books, on tape, in conversations—that will nurture my best inclinations and further my deepest interests?

♦ To whom can I give something that will matter? Where can I invest my energies today so that others will benefit and so that I, too, will grow and benefit? How can I make my giving most attractive, a unique offering that represents me well?

♦ Where in my life, home and personal affairs can I increase orderliness or make things neater and cleaner and work more efficiently?

There are several excellent texts on self-inquiry. One of the most useful is a book by Ira Progoff, titled *At a Journal Workshop*. I often recommend this book to people who are just starting out in journal-keeping. Progoff is a master teacher in the art of self-inquiry. He structures his journal-exercises so that the questions asked are open-ended, drawing upon the individual's inner knowledge and helping bring interior wisdoms to the surface of awareness.

Another excellent book is a classic (perhaps now hard to locate, although most libraries will have a copy) by David Seabury, titled *The Art of Selfishness*. I find that many contemporary "creativity workshops" must help people deal with their guilt before they can address creativity. Many people have been taught to feel guilty for doing what they most prefer, or they feel guilty for going against the wishes of others, or for simply wanting to be who they are. Seabury, writing in the 1930's, outlines what he calls a Basic Law of Being:

NEVER COMPROMISE YOURSELF. No matter what the situation, how pressing the problem, never give up your integrity. When you do, you make more sorrow than when you don't, hurting everyone in the end. (Seabury, 1974 ed., p. 5)

I like his advice because it is practical and stimulating. It helps me remember to limit my involvement to only those things that bring satisfaction to me. And in time others are served, too. If, for example, we like to garden, cook or participate in a certain community activity, then these are the things we must do. From these choices and efforts, others receive great value. But if we don't like to read, for example, there is no rule that says we must. Forcing ourselves to do something we really don't enjoy undermines whatever creative juices we have within us.

Another self-corrective activity that serves the creative process is that of bringing order into any part of life. I have found it especially helpful, when I am perplexed by a chapter I'm writing or confused by a professional problem, to pay greater attention to my housekeeping. We might think of this as a sort of "Zen of Housekeeping." For example, my linen closet might get my time one afternoon. I'll put everything else out of mind while I put sachets amongst the linens and arrange everything as neatly and aesthetically as possible. When I have quietly and mindfully attended to some physical chore such as this, my creative drive seems enhanced. Before long I am feeling excited about the new chapter, or I have answers to my business problem. I'm not sure why this works, but it always does. This reminds me of the Zen saying, "Nothing special." In other words, by paying heed to our ordinary actions, by doing these smaller things as meticulously and with as much concentration and presence as possible, eventually we do the larger activities more consciously.

Paying attention to the details of everyday life is a variation on the proverbial rule that when we take care of the small matters, the larger ones almost take care of themselves. As we expand the sphere of our self-correction, moving from smaller to larger areas of concern, we practice those same skills in both areas: those that are important to us and those that are unimportant. Since, in the smaller realms, we have taught ourselves to pay attention to our preferences, in the significant areas of life we will be capable, too. Seeing our capabilities increase gives rise to increased confidence and independence and this, in turn, allows creativity to blossom.

For those who have never considered themselves creative, bodywork, dance or physical movement work is ideal. The body grows rigid along with the mind. Also, as we begin to do something physical, we must face our own timidity about appearing foolish, about not-knowing how to do something. We watch ourselves grow frightened about what others will think of us. Or we notice that we are uncomfortable with the ambiguity of the task. Perhaps we are fearful to take risks. All these observations can help us become more creative if we persevere.

Creative persons enjoy taking small risks into the unknown. They are not particularly disturbed if they arouse other people's curiosity, humor or even disdain. Learning to dance is a perfect way to be foolish safely, while we explore and push back the boundaries of our willingness to take risks, to play, to deal with the unknown. This memory—of ourselves as being willing to be playful in the midst of our discomfort—can serve our other activities, just as the ordering of a kitchen cabinet helps put greater order into our more significant affairs. From dance, yoga, or even therapeutic massage, we find ways of moving into other creative arenas of life. It is not that this or that activity is more creative than another, but what we ourselves *bring* to the activity that counts as creative.

There is no end to this sort of learning. At any stage of life, and at all stages of development, we can push back the boundaries of what we cannot do, expanding the boundaries of what we *can* do. The more we know ourselves as capable, the more capable we become, and this capability involves itself in our greater resourcefulness as persons. Work, art, crafts, community projects, simple household or garden chores—these simply are places to begin exercising our independence, our more creative selves. We must start somewhere, and what better place than in these familiar ones?

As long as we keep on growing as a self, as long as we pursue our interests in meaningful projects and specifically those that will benefit future generations, our life-force persists. We will live—really *live*—until the end. I am reminded of a friend's father, in his late nineties, who, at this writing, is quite ill in the hospital. Of her father my friend said, "I don't know if he will make it this time. He said to me the other day that he'd done just about all he wants to do, that he is satisfied."

Perhaps there is a time for each of us to express our fulfillment and move on. Perhaps, as Helen Nearing said, we too will want to meet that time and place where we can "go on myself and see what's doing over there." The point is to live fully, vigorously and happily until the moment we are ready to go on.

7

Healing Skills
and Healing Choices

For he who would proceed aright . . . should begin in
youth to visit beautiful forms. . . . Soon he will of himself
perceive that the beauty of one form is akin to the beauty
of another, and that beauty in every form is one in the
same.

Plato
Symposium

I have been describing "healing" primarily as an inner mending
process: an interior phenomenon that knits us together as persons, integrating us so that, progressively, we become whole.
In this chapter I want to focus greater attention on how the
simplest of choice-making patterns, rooted in our good will,
might promote actual *physical healing*.

There is an overwhelming body of evidence coming out
of the medical field itself which shows that our daily choices
(especially our self-attitudes, routines and habits) affect our
physical health. Choice of diet, the regularity and quantity of
exercise, the quality of relationships, belief systems and life-
style as a whole—all of these choices seem to contribute either
to health or to dis-ease.

An obvious example of a choice that can keep us healthy
is choosing *not* to smoke. Nonsmokers enjoy greater health
benefits (such as clearer lungs and better cardiovascular sys-

tems) than smokers. The choice not to smoke has definite physical ramifications in our lives.

As another example of how choices affect health, I know a man who was not happy in his profession. He retired early, at age fifty-five. When he retired he seemed depressed and worn out. But, since then, because of the way he chooses to live each day, he has revitalized himself. He runs every day, rain or shine. He lives simply, has modified his diet to a low-fat, nonalcohol, high fiber one. He putters around his garden and house, reads in-between these gentle activities, and has greatly narrowed his circle of friends. Now he elects to spend time only with those he finds most supportive and interesting. He looks better, laughs more, seems settled inside himself. He tells me he sleeps like a baby—easily and peacefully. Aches and pains are gone. In sum, he apparently has lengthened his life by choosing to correct those things that were out of balance.

These are just two of many illustrations of how our choices can prevent illness. Furthermore, our choices can help us get well when we are ill. These are also "healing choices." Yet, because they are grounded in a specific way of being, I also think of these choices as *healing skills*, as abilities that let us interact healthfully with our environment and other people. And, over time, these skills help us develop a worldview, an approach to life, that is potent, life-affirming, energizing and life-promoting.

A CAUTION: NO NEED FOR GUILT

Before I get deeper into this topic of healing choices or healing skills, I must make it clear that I don't believe that all disease—whether simple, everyday illnesses or serious life-threatening ones—has psychological roots. Sometimes, as

Freud reputedly said, "A cold is just a cold." Sometimes, late in life for instance, our physical body may just wear out. My friend's father, mentioned briefly in the last chapter, is an example: at some point he sensed he lived long enough—I think he chose to move on naturally.

I bring this up because I see a dangerous tendency, especially among holistic health practitioners, to imply that people who have heart disease, ulcers, cancer and other ailments "create" their illnesses. It's as if they are somehow faulty as persons. While I don't deny that way of being, attitudes and interactive styles do affect our immune system and can produce illness, I am loath to see healers take too psychological an approach. This can produce shame and guilt, and these emotions are the last things the sick need.

An example of this stance is found in an otherwise very helpful book on nearsightedness I recently read. It describes the myopic character as emotionally isolated, perfectionistic, unspontaneous in humor, feeling incompetent (but competing anyway, then burying negative feelings) and so on.

Even though it is helpful to remember that strain, on any level of life, produces strains on our nerves, muscles and interior chemistry, including such things as hormone production which affects the intricate fluid balance in the eyes, at the same time, I know many myopic people who just do not fit the unattractive psychological mold suggested. They are spontaneous, humorous, competent and fun to be around. Genetic predispositions, early childhood experiences, each person's unique bio-chemistry—these also affect eye health. My myopic friends are artists and musicians, homemakers, scientists and business colleagues and most are outstanding in their field.

I also prefer to keep in mind that on the other side of all character "flaws" are certain benefits. The seemingly inflexible person may require stubborness to produce a life's work in science or art. The person who seems to lack spontaneous humor may, under the surface, have a more sophisticated idea of what is funny than we do. The gentle, quiet, person who appears "passive" to onlookers might use her gentle way to accomplish a great deal of good interpersonally. Perfectionists generally embody the highest standards of safety or precision in their work. And so on.

David Seabury, whose work I cited in the last chapter, advises us to associate a positive benefit with every negative trait we find in ourselves. He says:

> . . . think out and intimately associate a healthful dynamic behavior pattern with every unfortunate and destructive factor that is uncovered in [your] analysis of [yourself]. [You] can do more by this single control of attention than by all other procedures. (Seabury, 1974, p. 168)

Quite opposite to the guilt-inducing message is the message of love, taught by a physician I know. This seems to me the way to go. He recently initiated a support group for cancer patients in which the group's goal is total self-acceptance. They work at a discipline of self-acceptance in order to get well. They do not heap upon themselves still greater amounts of guilt for their supposedly illness-producing ways of being. My physician friend reports that when his patients allow themselves to *be* what they are, when they show this simple form of love and respect for themselves, they begin to feel better physically. Again I am reminded that the great healers of the past taught only love. Christ's comments to those who were healed in his presence was, "Your faith has made you well."

We do well to keep in mind that we are *beings in potentium*—we contain within us, in latent form, all traits, all attributes, all possibilities. It is up to us, at a particular point in time, to choose which trait, which attribute, which possibility to draw out and articulate.

In sum, it is more helpful to love ourselves as we are, instead of expecting ourselves to live up to an artificial ideal or profile, or to one specific behavioral description, imposed from without. And a final word: whole, healthy persons embody all opposites—they are brave and cowardly, rigid and flexible, serious and humorous, and, as Maslow wrote, "simultaneously worms and gods."

The quintessential challenge, when we are ill, is to take full responsibility for getting better. This necessarily includes surveying our typical response style, the stressors in our life, the way we have chosen to adapt, emote, strive, avoid or greet challenge and so forth. This also means examining our belief system to see if, within ourselves, we have a securely implanted notion that says we *can* get well. We must have this idea in place if we are to become what has been termed "high level wellness" persons. If this notion is not firmly in place, we do ourselves great good by saturating our minds with literature, tapes and research material that supports the cause of self-healing. The mind/body link is a sound one, but we should use this link to get better, not to blame ourselves for our illness.

WHAT ARE HEALING SKILLS

Having inserted that caution, I now add that there *are* things we can do to take better care of ourselves. While we do more harm than good by blaming ourselves for lack of health, we can and must be responsible for our well-being: emotional and physical. This paradox weaves through this entire subject. Thus what follows is not meant to be taken in a self-critical light; rather I hope to tip the information scale so that each person can use what follows to stay well, get better if ill, and keep an ever-watchful eye on his or her mind's messages and beliefs as relates to wellness.

It may be helpful to approach the topic of healing by looking at certain choices as *skills*. We can develop any skill, while continuing to be whoever we are now. That is, without subjecting ourselves to inordinate negative self-analysis or the intrusive analysis of others who would define us, we can objectively scan our behavior, attitudes and beliefs so as to simultaneously strengthen whatever self-supports we have and correct whatever undermines us at present. If we cling tenaciously, for instance, to our individual fighting spirit, we protect ourselves from the definitions of others. At the same time we must cultivate a loving flexibility to grow and develop in optimum directions. We might think of this procedure as an *additive process:* we are adding needed skills and choice-patterns, rather than over-analyzing ourselves or hating ourselves for being one way or another. Thomas Merton in a short work on Saint Bernard wrote that in the process of resolving our contradictions we become whole. This comes closest to the mark of what I suggest in these paragraphs.

A specific healing skill, already touched upon, is the ability to accept ourselves as we are. Self-acceptance gives us the strength to get better if we're ill and to stay well if we're fit. Self-acceptance joins us together at the very point of rupture. This helps, however subtly, resolve contradiction.

Other healing skills include *assertiveness* and *self-awareness*. For instance, sometimes we must defend ourselves when others (family members, doctors, bureaucracies) intrude upon our rights, our privacy or our desire for information. In these instances, we need to be plainspoken about what we know we need and want for ourselves: we honestly stand up for ourselves even when it goes against other people's advice. This ability, this skill, is learnable; it involves a complex of sub-skills, assertiveness and self-awareness being two of them.

There are many parallels between healing skills and what I call *creative adaptive skills*, a diagnostic term I've coined for another book I'm writing on this general subject (Sinetar, 1989). Creative adaptive skills are those behaviors that help people flourish, despite personal setback or crises. While creative adaptive skills apply to any major life changes or traumas, many similarities exist between this and the healing skills needed to overcome grave illness. Returning to my earlier remarks, it is clear to me that self-blame, excessive analysis and guilt are maladaptive factors when we are ill.

I have found that creative adaptive skills are comprised of synergistic behavior clusters that reinforce each other. As one skill is exercised and developed, the other two are enhanced. Thus, these skill-sets depend upon each other, hence are *synergistic*. This quality of synergism also holds true for healing skills.

As an example, one woman, who described herself as "overcommitted," spoke about her choice to get more control over her life. For her this choice was summed up in a phrase she affirmed to herself: "Slow down." She knew if she didn't pull back on many levels, her well-being would be in jeopardy. Her backaches and headaches brought her to a physician, who told her the same thing: slow down. She described herself in this way:

> I said "Yes" to everything and everyone. I tried to please everyone. I was out of balance, and life wasn't working. To gain control, I just tried to slow down. I took more time for myself every morning. I chose to say "no" to extraneous activities. I taught myself over a period of months that the world wouldn't end if I didn't accomplish everything quickly.

> The result? My headaches stopped. I began to sleep better. My backaches are completely gone. In the process, I

realized I thought better of myself and felt more excited about what I could do with my life. The quality of my life improved so much.

Indeed, positive self-feelings do emerge when we take control of our lives. Negative self-feelings stem from choices that leave us at the effect of other people and outer circumstances. This woman got more control over her life by putting her need for a simpler, slower life first. And as she did this she gained control of her life in general. She also gained feelings of self-worth. Had she dwelt upon her hyperactivity, had she spent too much time in self-blame for her out-of-balance life, she could have easily discounted her ability to act in a new, more effective manner.

Controlling our thoughts, actions and emotions—especially if we are ill—is difficult. But this may be the choice-pattern that helps us believe in ourselves, value our life and feel we have a chance to get better. Research suggests that people who get well despite life-threatening illnesses, unlike those who do not, may be more assertive—perhaps even hostile at times.

This makes sense. When overly compliant, we find it impossible to ignore our physician's predictions about our chances for survival. His or her words ring loud in us. If these predictions are dismal, our own hope erodes the longer we pay attention. In the last chapter, we saw that hope helps us endure. But in order to sustain hope or optimism in the face of morbid predictions, when statistics work against us, we must firmly shut out negative news, keep dominant our most positive thoughts and emotions, and fiercely kindle our own life-fuel so that we *can* make it. However, ignoring negative comments is nearly impossible when we want to please others, when we put their voice over our inner voice.

Furthermore, if we are too compliant, too "nice," we then ignore our own preferences (even though we are furious beneath the surface), going along with other people's wishes instead. Even when healthy, we so easily undermine ourselves if we are always docile. Then we listen to, and obey, our parents' injunctions. We obey other dominant adults. We marry someone whom others value, or enter occupations they think worthwhile. The variations on this theme are endless. The point is this: if we do not exercise our will for our own preferences, we find ourselves overwhelmed with advice from well-meaning others when ill.

Choosing to stay in control of our life I call a healing *skill*. There are countless ways to choose that let us take control over our thoughts and emotions and even circumstances. This skill activates our fighting spirit, a natural partner to robust physical health.

People whom Dr. Bernie Siegel describes as "bad" patients have a fighting spirit. "Good" patients are those who don't ask too many questions, go along with their doctor's wishes and medications, believe what they're told, don't make waves. By contrast, "bad" patients are expressive. They cry when hurt. They ask tough questions. They become enraged and hostile when it's warranted, for example if they're frustrated by pat or evasive answers or when they become entangled in red tape. They follow the old adage, "I don't get headaches, I give them."

Furthermore, bad patients see themselves as equal partners with doctors in the healing process. They do not see themselves as defective, a step or two beneath physicians as persons or intellectually inferior. In his book *Love, Medicine and Miracles* Siegel reports that a group of London researchers found a ten-year survival rate of seventy-nine percent among "bad" cancer patients, compared to only a twenty-two percent survival rate among those who were "good." Interesting enough, they had a greater number of killer T cells—the white cells that seek out and destroy cancer cells. (Siegel, 1987)

Bad patients might leave a hospital against their doctor's orders. They often refuse a traditional treatment. There is great risk here: they could grow worse, even die. But their commitment is to life, to their own life-spirit, and they are willing to take that risk. They possess creative, experimental drive, a sort of "let's see what happens if I do this" posture. This stance breeds and cultivates risk-tolerance which in turn allows people to have more comfort while in ambiguous situations. To choose wisely against conventional wisdom takes skill. There are risks each time we choose in this fashion. We can develop our skill by practicing, and preferably by practicing in low-risk areas of life.

No one illustrates the skills of self-affirmation and risk-taking better than does author Norman Cousins. In his book *Anatomy of an Illness*, and later in *The Healing Heart*, Cousins describes how, when faced with grave illness, he became convinced that the hospital was no place for a sick person. While he was in the hospital, he put up signs on his hospital door, telling hospital staff what treatments he would and would not accept. Later he moved to a hotel room so that he could continue his preferred treatment program: massive doses of vitamin C and classic comedic movies that made him laugh and feel more optimistic.

Cousins was a "bad" patient. As another example, when he noticed that four different hospital technicians from four different departments were taking blood for tests they wished to run, he decided not to go along:

> Taking four large slugs of blood the same day, even from a healthy person, is hardly to be recommended. When the technicians came the second day to fill their containers with blood . . . I turned them away and had a sign posted

on my door saying that I would give just one specimen
every three days, and that I expected the different departments to draw from one vial for their individual needs.
(Cousins, 1979, p. 29)

In another inspiring book, Cousin's physicians note that
their suggestions were filtered through his own judgment
mechanisms. One doctor, for example, who knew Cousins was
in pain during his first illness—a serious bout with collagen
disease—recommended that he not play tennis so vigorously,
perhaps give it up entirely. Cousins knew that he got tremen-
dous pleasure out of the sport; his body needed the vigorous
workout. So, despite pain, he pressed on. Dr. Omar Fareed
tells us that this turns out to have been the healing choice:

We didn't know it at the time, but his brain was probably
releasing endorphins, the body's own painkilling secretions. It is interesting, as I look at it now, that he should
have been the beneficiary of those secretions that later
served as the basis of his work and studies at UCLA. (Cousins, 1983, p. 267)

Cousin's choice-making all the way along the line of his
illnesses reconditioned his body. But he had to go against his
physicians' advice, and he actively questioned *each* hospital
procedure as he faced it, in order to get well. Somewhere
within himself he knew what he needed—although it may have
been the softest sense or hunch. He risked all—his very life—
in order to pursue this sense of what turned out to be a better,
and a healing, way. This is what I call "staying in control."

His books demonstrate that he employed a cluster of healing skills to maintain control, among them self-awareness, self-
acceptance, assertiveness, and creativity.

There are countless choices we might make so as to qualify as "bad" patients. Bernie Siegel provides a long list in his

book; among his suggestions: bring meditation tapes to the hospital and listen to them frequently, decorate your room with favorite memorabilia, insist that your room have a view—no view of brick walls tolerated, and so on. These choices reinstate feelings of power in circumstances where hospital bureaucracy constantly evades it. As noted in my earliest remarks, giving, cooperation with others, and service—or what some have come to call "stewardship"—are also healing *skills*. When we give to others out of love, in an unconditional way, we are simultaneously giving a high quality love to ourselves. This energy carries with it a miracle power which may have special properties, healing properties. Can we love ourselves when we are ill? Can we embrace our own fear and anxieties? Can we forgive those who have hurt us in the past? I believe that our ability to *live* our highest emotion—love—in our choices and daily attitudes can heal us.

A MATTER OF PRACTICE

If we first take on lesser, low-risk battles, we are better able to make choices that let us take control when we face high-risk situations. If we first practice in life's innocuous areas, we then arm ourselves with the skills we need to meet difficult challenges later. One practice method I suggest is simple observation: find people who are good at the thing you want to do and watch them.

A friend of mine, a vice-president in a major corporation, is excellent at practicing control-skills. Her company is an intricate, enormous web of bureaucracy. It is standard procedure for each department head to distribute reams and reams of forms to executives to be filled out in triplicate. My friend throws all forms away. She refuses to occupy herself with massive paperwork (although filling out these forms is required by her company). Yet she is respected as one of that company's more creative people. Indeed, she displays creativity in both major and minor ways—not only by refusing to waste time on voluminous, quite unnecessary paperwork. She has added time to think ingeniously *because* she chooses creatively each time an option is presented.

Another illustration of what I mean by "practice control skills" comes from my own experience. I once visited a hospital for minor surgery where the receptionist greeted me with a lengthy form. The small print at the bottom of the form said that the hospital would not perform the surgery without every question completed fully. Several questions were obviously marketing ones, such as blanks for the patient's yearly income and highest level of schooling. I felt that these were irrelevant to my surgery and none of the hospital's business. I left these spaces blank.

When I returned the form, the receptionist coolly pointed out that I had failed to answer all the questions. Imperially she told me that there would be no surgery without my completing the form. I told her (with several degrees' greater coolness) that if surgery were denied me on the basis of my not answering those questions, the hospital would be guilty of an unconstitutional act. (I didn't know *what* act, I just knew that level of income or education had nothing to do with their performing surgery.) The receptionist was stunned. A staff gathering ensued. The clerks and nurses— finally a doctor—solemnly discussed matters. I hummed a few bars of "Dixie" and pretended not to care. After a few minutes, with a decidedly different tone, the receptionist returned to say that they had ruled in my favor. They would grant me surgery without knowing what grade in school I had completed. It's not hard to find such obvious and enjoyable battles in which to practice risk-taking, assertion, and the muscles of one's fighting spirit.

CONTROL BUT NOT CONTROLLING

Clearly, to stay in control of life, we must draw a line over which others may not cross. If we do not, we will be mistreated, victimized and put upon.

But in order to stay in charge, it is imperative that we not be *controlling*. In other words, we must also be able to relinquish control. Being in control and being controlling are entirely different matters.

Letting go—the ability to let something (or ourselves) be, the willingness to die, if we must, on behalf of life—is also a healing skill. If we attempt to control others, if we require guarantees, if we clutch at life desperately, then we do not *live*.

When we cling to life, we live half-heartedly. We become overly cautious, uncommitted; we waver at each fork in the road. By comparison, when we fully embrace life, we live all-out—as if life mattered, were valued to the hilt, as if we could die at any moment. The person who throws out meaningless forms, the one who tells a hospital how much blood they may take from his veins, those who refuse to answer questions just because they are asked—these are all persons also willing to have the tide go against them. These are responsible choosers who know they may pay for their choices with dire consequences—the loss of a job in one case, the loss of life in another, and so forth.

But if we are unwilling to accept the consequences of our actions and choices, we never really live. The one who stays at a deadening job because he or she fears change lives half a life. People who are vigorously engaged in life are less likely to experience the nameless fears or free-floating anxieties of those who live marginally, on the threshold but never completely *in* life. Only independent self-sufficient persons, realizing there are risks to everything, choose freely, then stand by their choice.

I interviewed a woman who, due to breast cancer, agreed to undergo chemotherapy and a radical mastectomy. She insisted upon working throughout her illness, although of course she did miss some work. Her family advised against staying on the job. They were afraid she would tax herself unnecessarily. They feared for her life. Only her husband was supportive. He knew that her work comprised a great deal of her life, that it meant independence, involvement and dignity for her. He supported her choice. They both knew she was taking a risk. Here is what she said of her decision:

> I didn't know if working would help me or hurt me. All I knew was that my job was meaningful. If I died, so be it. I just didn't want to live a meaningless life—not for a minute, especially not when life, every minute and day of it, had become so precious to me. I had to trust and let go. I believe I'm here today, talking with you, because I could do that.

As soon as we embrace our own death, confront it head-on, live in a way that says, "I love my life enough to live it meaningfully," then we live all-out. Letting go is part of the life-process. But even here there are no guarantees.

The irony is this: to be truly in control, we must let go. The person who trusts, the person who feels subjectively safe, the one who has faith, lets go. All others cling. People who meditate or pray understand this irony from experience. Before meditating, we first calm our body and mind enough so that letting go is possible. Only then do we slip into an effortless state of being, where the "breath breathes us." Here, in this state, there is a complete release of tension and strain. Here thinking ceases. But we can never arrive at this level of consciousness if we "try" to, if we are overly controlling, if we refuse to let go.

Those who enjoy dancing also understand: until our bodies and muscles warm up, when we first start dancing, we feel stiff, move clumsily. We may be self-conscious or try to re-create a new dance step we've seen someone else do. Whatever we do, while efforting, while self-conscious, while trying to control our feet, we don't actually dance. We exist outside the music. But after a while, we stop thinking. The music, the steps, our foolish appearance—these cease to matter. We just dance. We become music, we are dance. Because we give up control, music and dance take us over.

To let go in this fashion, whether in dance, in meditation or in life, we must surrender to something beyond ourselves. Surrender seems our point of power.

Although no one has ever been able to say "why" this is so, miracles happen when we relinquish control. The point of relinquishment is where we release our faith. Fear disappears and a higher quality of love takes over in our bodies and minds. Nietzsche, quoted earlier, wrote that life's secret is that it must ever surpass itself. When we let go, when we die to ourselves, we are surpassed, born into a larger life, a greater experience of who we are. Perhaps this is what dying "correctly," in the physical sense, really is all about. If so, then heaven surely means larger life.

When we commit ourselves to something beyond ourselves—life itself, a particular work, idea or truth, a sacred value—we act out of the highest level of personal responsibility. Here we are somehow set free. The box we have been in, limiting us as persons, opens and we experience our true humanity, our true life.

This is tricky for me to explain. Christ's example during his last hour helps. Certainly he suffered. Surely he desired to live. Nevertheless he accepted, even embraced, his death in a way that transmuted its sting, turned its negative power into something divine. Why cannot we do the same, especially with the smaller trials that come our way?

One possible answer is that we lack sufficient strength and commitment to things larger than ourselves. Christ's example teaches a critical lesson. He teaches anyone willing to take notice—Christian and non-Christian alike. He seized and mastered the moment, completely accepting that trial, head-on. His absolute truthfulness to an impeccable standard of virtue, even at this last, most painful moment of life, made him so fully alive that he transcended death. Salvation, taught Kierkegaard, exists only in the purity with which we will the Good. In willing the Good, each and every time, we find we must let go—love, give, accept with a hand open to the moment and the unknown. This absolute commitment *is* life.

Dietrich Bonhoeffer, the young German pastor who was executed by the Nazis for his active, unrelenting resistance to that regime, talks of the type of commitment and singleminded courage which "lets go" in a similar fashion. This all-out commitment enlarges and elevates us, even (and especially) during moments of crisis or trauma.

In *The Costs of Discipleship*, Bonhoeffer maintains that absolute faithfulness enables us to meet any earthly test with strength. Such faithfulness means total concentration and the orientation of one's whole life toward a superordinate goal. Such goals differ, depending on the person. Bonhoeffer's goal was to live as a disciple of Christ. Christ's goal was to do God's will. The goal of the woman who survived breast cancer was to live meaningfully, to the end, even if this resulted in her death. Our fixed commitment must be to that which is larger than ourselves; this liberates us. This has healing power.

I believe that the concentration of a committed heart releases energy with curative powers. Healing choices are committed, though not necessarily forced, choices: choosing to accept ourselves, choosing to live according to the highest standards of virtue or self-treatment, choosing to do battle with those who would undermine our life, choosing to abandon people and circumstances toxic to our well-being, choosing to live aesthetically, can all be healing choices if done with consciousness and commitment. Commitment grounds us in love, and therefore is capable of making us well.

I also believe there is a place for medicine, doctors and surgeries as we traditionally know them. God works through many people, not just through us. Bernie Siegel relates the story of a man who is told he has cancer and is going to die. The man prays to God, asking direction. God answers, "I will save you." The man, feeling comforted, refuses the surgery that his doctor assures him is the only way to be saved. The man dies. In heaven, he confronts God and asks, "What happened? You promised me I'd live." God answers, "I sent a surgeon to you in your final hour. Why didn't you take advantage of *my* gift?"

This story aside, there are also numerous ways we can help ourselves. Whether in illness or in day-to-day life, we have the power and the responsibility to choose on our own behalf. We can choose to speak up when we feel put upon or discounted. We can choose to live, on a daily basis, out of the highest standard of ethics, aesthetics or health. We can monitor our thoughts so that we don't plague ourselves with unproductive, negative, discouraging ideas. We can demonstrate generosity, toward ourselves and others. We can practice being honest with ourselves by keeping a journal, or by simply speaking forthrightly and truthfully to friends and family.

By maintaining our integrity in the little ways, we teach ourselves to have integrity as a person. There are endless choices we can make—most of them inconsequential in and of themselves—by which we commit ourselves to what is good. We can choose to develop our own "good will." That means that we exercise our mind and will so as to delight in virtue, truth, beauty and other positive values. In other words, we commit ourselves to what is, to us, *the good*.

SUMMARY

I promised at the outset to be practical. Yet how does one commit specifically to the Good? The principle seems so vague, so goody-two-shoes nebulous. A correspondence I had recently with a friend may help me explain this practice: my friend wrote saying that he could not forgive himself for failing to stand up publicly for a man he greatly admired. He felt ashamed, said he had betrayed the other man, had gone against his own right-ethic. He said he did not know how to repair the damage.

I wrote him the following reply:

> You are very hard on yourself. One sure cure for self-for-giveness is for you to locate someone who has done to you what you feel you have done to another. Forgive him. That will surely clear you out at the same time. It is hard, but it works for me each and every time.

> Another thing: ask yourself how you would talk to a be-loved child of yours, say, a son of six or seven, if he had been too frightened of some nameless thing to speak up as he felt he 'should.' To your son you would be kind and helpful. So reassuring. But to yourself you are so harsh. Talk to yourself that way. This is a good time to practice.

We are too hard on ourselves. To heal, we must stop this. But because we have not developed sufficient loving strength, we do not stand up for ourselves, or others, when we most need and want to. Then—without courage, without loving strength—we cave in. We accept our own or others' harsh judgment or toxic treatment. We notice how open, how receptive we are to their mistreatment. This observation registers. Later, we punish ourselves in devastatingly subtle ways: a vicious cycle. We can stop this cycle by loving ourselves, by committing ourselves to our own good. This, as I have attempted to describe in these pages, is done by expressing our highest virtue in every choice. When our true values, virtues and competencies flow through us, whatever the choice, then transformative power—life-power—is ours as well. We are enlivened, as is everything our choice touches.

Choices and life as a whole are inseparable. What we choose to *be* is reflected in our thoughts, our words, our actions—even in our choice of friends and associates. These add up to become what we ourselves are, as persons.

The choices I describe as healing have a common denominator: they allow our real self, what some call our "ground of being," to emerge. However shyly and hesitatingly this coreself comes into existence, it charms us; it brilliantly illumines our life for the better.

Every good act registers in us, although usually unconsciously, and makes us love and respect ourselves. This in itself is reason enough to stay awake about choice-making. Healing choices embody any, or all, of these characteristics:

♦ They are consciously made. We notice what we have done. Despite any struggle or hardship along the way, the result somehow pleases us. We know and say in ourselves, "This is for the best. This is good. I'm glad I did this. This is one of the best things I've ever done."

♦ These are virtuous choices. As Kierkegaard put it, we will the Good. Our own purity and goodness shines through these choices, even if only to us. Eventually our Good "flows" through us.

♦ These choices demonstrate commitment to our own core-self; the values and desires of the real self grow and are revealed.

♦ These choices express and let us better understand our own personal aesthetic: how we like to do things, what we stand for, what we find pleasing, necessary and life-enhancing. In time, there is flow to our choices; the choices themselves become symbolic of some essential aspect of our core-self.

♦ The Being Values—truth, honor, courage, humility, patience, order, compassion, and especially love (for self, for others, forgiveness, etc.)—are expressed through these choices.

Perhaps we can overdo this. We can over-analyze this subject, intellectualize it to death. To do so would be to kill the very spirit I am talking about. But done rightly, giving greater attention to the good in a mindful, consistent and quietly unobtrusive way fills us with self-respect and healing energy. Attending to our good in the way I have described seems much the way of all great and inspiring persons. Gandhi's notes, personal letters and life-choices, for example, were full of this type of attention to the morally and aesthetically elevated choice:

> I know the path: it is straight and narrow. It is like the edge of a sword. I rejoice to walk on it. I weep when I slip. God's word is: He who strives never perishes. I have implicit faith in that promise. Though, therefore, from my weakness I fail a thousand times, I will not lose faith. (Gandhi, 1980, p. 66)

When we live in this way, as we pay attention to our choices, we come into the present. The details of each act become important, but not so dominant as to mesmerize us. Overall, we grow more conscious daily, infinitely better equipped to observe the consequences and meaning of our choices and then adapt effectively. We grow personally more powerful, in the sense that we become *able* to do what we need, want and value to do.

We also become better readers of our own choice-patterns. Decidedly there are messages in our choices, feedback systems that reveal us to ourselves. When we are sloppy, rushed or anxious, we notice. When things work smoothly, we notice. We learn what works for, and against, us. As awareness and understanding grow, we grow. In time, with practice and commitment, we become refined choice-makers, gracefully active authors of our lives.

Ironically, we are then better able to release ourselves fully to the *demands* of the moment. Most significantly, the more comprehensive and universal our awareness—a phenomenon of awareness which occurs with being fully present—the more potent our choices. We gain control, while somehow "emptying" ourselves. We possess full control, but with a measure of interior trust and faith that allow us to let go, to just *be*. *To be*, in this fashion, whatever our circumstances, is elegant. For this is life, real power and true health.

Be assured, I am far from living this way of being myself. There are moments, it is true, and these are bliss, and these point me along the course of which I write. Although these moments grow, I do not want to come across as something I am not. But I sense this to be the exact direction of the work. I practice daily.

References

Allen, Woody. *Rolling Stone*. Issue 487, April 9, 1987.

Bonhoeffer, Dietrich. *The Cost of Discipleship*. New York: Macmillan, 1963.

Bucke, Richard. *Cosmic Consciousness*. New York: E.P. Dutton & Co., 1969.

Byrom, Thomas. *The Dhammapada*. New York: Vintage Books, 1976.

Cantwell-Kiley, John. *Self-Rescue*. New York: Fawcett-Crest, 1977.

Chesterton, G.K. *Saint Francis of Assisi*. New York: Image Books, 1957.

Clark, Etta. *Growing Old Is Not For Sissies*. Corta Madera, California: Pomogranet Books, 1986.

Colwin, Laurie. *Happy All the Time*. Harrisonburg: R.R. Donnelley & Sons, 1978.

Costas, Christ. "The Irrepressible Helen Nearing." *East-West Magazine*. November, 1986.

Cousins, Norman. *Anatomy of an Illness*. New York: W. W. Norton, 1979.

————. *The Healing Heart*. New York: W. W. Norton, 1983.

Cowley, Malcom. *The View from 80*. New York: Viking Press, 1980.

Crisp, Quentin. *How To Have a Lifestyle*. New York: Methuen, Inc., 1979.

Dworkin, Andrea. *Ice and Fire*. New York: Weidenfeld & Nicolson, 1986.

Gandhi, M.K. *All Men Are Brothers*. New York: Continuum Publishing, 1980.

Goertzel, Victor and Mildred G. *Cradles of Eminence*. Canada: Little, Brown & Co., 1962.

Grundin, Robert. *Time and the Art of Living*. New York: Harper & Row, 1982.

Hartman, Franz. *The Life and Doctrines of Jacob Boehme*. New York: Macoy Publishing, 1929.

Howes, E. and Moon, S. *The Choicemaker*. Wheaton, Illinois: Quest Books Theosophical Publications, 1973.

Jung, Carl. *Modern Man in Search of a Soul*. New York: Harcourt, Brace & World, 1933.

Kierkegaard, Soren. *Purity of Heart*. New York: Harper & Row, 1938.

Kunkel, Fritz. *How Character Develops*. New York: Scribner, 1940.

Lindner, Robert. *Prescription for Rebellion*. New York: Grove Press, 1952.

Maslow, Abraham, *Toward a Psychology of Being*. New Jersey: D. Van Nostrand, Inc., 1962.

Merton, Thomas. *Life and Holiness*. New York: Image Books, 1964.

———. *The New Man*. Farrar, Straus & Giroux, 1961.

Perls, F.S. *Ego, Hunger and Aggression*. New York: Vintage Books, 1969.

Phillips, D., Howes, E. and Nixon, L. *Choice Is Always Ours*. Wheaton, Illinois: Re-Quest Books, 1977.

Saint Augustine, *On Free Choice of the Will*. Indianapolis: The Bobbs-Merrill Co., Inc., 1964.

Salinger, J.D. *Nine Stories*. New York: Bantam Books, 1953.

Seabury, David. *The Art of Selfishness*. New York: Vintage Books 1974.

Shainess, Natalie. *Sweet Suffering: Woman as Victim.* New York: Pocket Books, 1984.

Siegel, Bernie. *Love, Medicine and Miracles.* New York: Harper & Row, 1987.

Sinetar, Marsha. *Do What You Love, The Money Will Follow.* New Jersey: Paulist Press, 1987.

———. "Entrepreneurs, Chaos and Creativity." Sloans Management Review (MIT). Winter, 1985.

———. *Ordinary People as Monks and Mystics.* New Jersey: Paulist Press, 1986.

———. *Your Creative Options.* Work in progress, 1989.

Smith, Logan Pearsall. *All Trivia.* New York: Harcourt Brace & Co., 1934.

Szasz, Thomas. *The Second Sin.* Garden City: Anchor Press/ Doubleday, 1974.

Tammaro and Koontz. *The View from the Top of the Mountain.* Danville, Indiana: Barnyard Press Cooperative, Inc., 1981.

Torrance, E. Paul. *Guiding Creative Talent.* Englewood Cliffs, New Jersey: Prentice-Hall, 1962.

Tsunetomo, Yamamoto. *Hagakure: Book of the Samurai.* Tokyo, New York, San Francisco: Kodansha International Ltd., 1979.

Viscott, David. *Language of Feelings.* New York: Pocket Books, 1976.

Wood, Garth. *The Myth of Neurosis.* New York: Harper & Row, 1983.

About the Author

Marsha Sinetar is a leading exponent of the practical value of self-actualization. Long immersed in the study of creatively-gifted, spiritually-emerging adults, her findings are published in several books increasingly used worldwide in colleges and universities, by therapists and spiritual directors, and by spiritual seekers from diverse traditions. Dr. Sinetar began her career as a teacher and moved rapidly through the ranks of public education as a principal, curriculum specialist and university lecturer. In 1980, after earning a Ph.D. in psychology, she founded her own corporate psychology firm (Santa Rosa, California) and for years has advised top management of Fortune 500 corporations on issues of leadership and rapid organizational change. Marsha Sinetar presently lives "as quietly as possible" at her home among the coastal redwoods of the Pacific northwest.